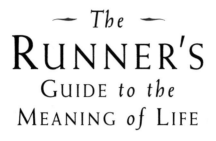

— *The* —

RUNNER'S
GUIDE *to the*
MEANING *of* LIFE

~ The ~
RUNNER'S
GUIDE *to the*
MEANING *of* LIFE

WHAT 35 YEARS OF RUNNING HAS TAUGHT
ME ABOUT WINNING, LOSING, HAPPINESS,
HUMILITY, AND THE HUMAN HEART

AMBY BURFOOT

WINNER OF THE 1968 BOSTON MARATHON
AUTHOR OF *THE PRINCIPLES OF RUNNING*
AND *RUNNER'S WORLD COMPLETE BOOK OF RUNNING*

DAYBREAK

Guides to the Meaning of Life is a trademark and *Daybreak* is a registered
trademark of Rodale Inc.

Printed in the United States of America on acid-free ∞, recycled paper ♻

Series Designer: Susan P. Eugster
Cover Designer: Stephanie M. Tarone
Cover Illustrator: Nip Rogers

Library of Congress Cataloging-in-Publication Data

Burfoot, Amby.
     The runner's guide to the meaning of life : what 35 years of running
has taught me about winning, losing, happiness, humility, and the
human heart / Amby Burfoot.
          p.   cm.
     ISBN 1–57954–263–8   hardcover
     1. Runners—Conduct of life.   2. Running—Philosophy.   3. Burfoot,
Amby.   I. Title.
GV1061.B792   2000
796.42—dc21   99–089556

Distributed to the book trade by St. Martin's Press

2 4 6 8 10 9 7 5 3 1 hardcover

Visit us on the Web at www.rodalebooks.com,
or call us toll-free at (800) 848-4735.

───── OUR PURPOSE ─────
*We publish books that empower
people's minds and spirits.*

DAYBREAK

Contents

Acknowledgments

When I first began running high school cross-country in the 1960s, I thought it was all about speed and endurance. When I moved on to college, I knew this for sure.

Please forgive me my mistakes.

As runners, we all go through many transitions—transitions that closely mimic the larger changes we experience in a lifetime. First, we try to run faster. Then we try to run farther. Then we learn to accept ourselves and our limitations, and at last, we can appreciate the true joy and meaning of running.

It's not about how fast you go. It's not about how far you go. It's a process. As we run, we become. Every workout reveals new truths and releases new dreams.

I'm not making this up. I've heard thousands of runners tell essentially the same story: "After I finished the marathon, I finally had the courage to start my new business." "After I lost 30 pounds on my running program, I signed up for evening classes at the local community college." "After my heart attack, I thought my life was over, but running gave me a new outlook on everything."

Listening to these testimonials, I began to reflect one day on how the lessons of running have so often helped me in my own life. And to think that the same lessons could help many others. Thus was this book born.

The book was written on the run, of course. That's when the best thoughts always bubble to the surface.

But it wasn't written alone. Most of the lessons contained herein were passed along to me by those I have known best and loved most in my life.

They are, of course, Mom and Dad. Gary and Natalie. Cristina and Dan and Laura. Ivy and Bill and George and Elmer and Jimmy and Jeffrey and an amazing number of Johns.

And beyond these, hundreds of friends and mentors and supporters. Thanks to all. Without you, my miles would have been empty indeed, and I would have found little meaning in this journey called life.

With you, my days have felt rich and fulfilling.

lesson one

Why Run?

I can barely see anymore. The salty sweat digging into my eyes stings so badly that I blink and blink, trying to get rid of it. Overhead, the sun shines so hot that it seems to be pouring molten lava over us. I force my hazy vision to focus on the bare shoulders just 2 yards in front of me. If only I can keep up. If only I can keep up.

The shoulders belong to John J. Kelley. He's my coach and mentor and inspiration, but most of all, right now, his shoulders are about the only thing between me and complete collapse.

We've already covered 12 miles on this sultry

1

July day. Only 4 more to go. But those 4 include a
2-mile sprint beside the Mystic River, a ½-mile as-
sault on aptly named Cliff Street, and a 1½-mile
charge through a tricky, twisting forest trail in the
Pequot Woods. The trail will end at our final desti-
nation, Kelley's backyard.

I'm exhausted, dehydrated, and overheated.
My prospects don't look good. I don't think I can
keep up. And I'm wondering: Why am I doing this?
Why do I run?

It's a question I will hear more than any other
in the next 4 decades. It's a question every runner
asks himself or herself a million times. And it's a
question that must be answered, or we cannot continue being runners, athletes, and adventurers.

Luckily for me, Kelley will disclose his answer
in a mere 30 minutes. Only I don't know that now,
as we race down Mystic River Road. I only know
that my will is fading, and my legs are turning to
rubber.

On Cliff Street, I can't keep up anymore.
Kelley begins pulling away from me, his blond hair

bobbing as his short but powerful legs churn up the steep hillside. I feel like quitting, but I don't. Runners don't quit. We fade; we "hit the wall"; we're sometimes reduced to a walk. But we keep on.

In the Pequot Woods, I lose sight of Kelley entirely on the curvy path. He's around the corner and far ahead of me now. I concentrate on my survival, looking down for branches, stones, streambeds. One false step, and I'll tumble head over heels. Tired as I am, it will take a long time to get up.

Somehow I manage to stay on my feet, and eventually I stumble into Kelley's backyard. He probably beat me there by 5 minutes, maybe 10. At any rate, he's showing no signs of the bone-crushing 16-mile training run we've just completed. He has stripped off his shirt and shoes, grabbed a shovel, and immediately commenced work on the vast organic garden that occupies most of his backyard.

He's spreading compost around the garden, heaving it to the far corner where the pole beans climb up carefully placed stakes. I am stunned by the thick, brown earthworms, hundreds of them, in every shovel of compost. Next, Kelley administers to the tomato plants, checking them for slug damage. As he does, and as I struggle to recover from the run, he begins to muse about the tensions between modern man and the eternal, relentless cycles of Nature.

He says that we are out of sync. We have forgotten, Kelley argues with Irish wit and relish, that we members of the species *Homo sapiens* are only recently evolved from the apes and their predecessors. We have moved too quickly away from the earth that sustains us; we have grown blind to our true animal selves. We have too many machines and chemicals, and we don't exercise enough. "How can automobiles and TVs make us better or healthier?" he sputters.

Still a teenager, I filled to the brim with Kelley's words. I have never forgotten them, and I have always tried to live by them. Sure, I have a car and a TV, but I also have an organic garden and a daily exercise habit, and the latter are far more important to me than the former.

Kelley taught me half the answer to the question, Why run? And that is: I run because I am an animal. I run because it is part of my genetic wiring. I run because millions of years of evolution have left me programmed to run. And, finally, I run because there's no better way to see the sun rise and set.

It took me many years to learn the other half of the answer.

What the years have shown me is that running clarifies the thinking process as well as purifies the body. I think best—most broadly and most fully— when I am running.

I know a Yale professor who has attempted to explain why we think so well when we run. He says that it's because running is an "undifferentiated activity." Sounds like professor talk, doesn't it?

Here's what I think he means: You don't need any skill to run. In golf, by contrast, you have to hit your drives straight enough to stay in the fairway, and that requires thinking about a dozen technical details of your golf swing. In tennis, you'd better master the backhand stroke, or your rallies will be short. In swimming . . . well, you'll drown if you don't develop some skills.

Not so with running. Every 3-year-old knows how to run. At the same time, running is the most vigorous exercise known to science. It forces your heart to pump vast quantities of blood throughout your body—including your brain. So the brain's getting all this oxygen at a time when it doesn't have any work to do. You're just running. You're not putting together business plans, solving quadratic equations, or trying to keep your drive from slicing off the fairway.

No wonder the brain spins out the most fantastical thoughts while you're running. No wonder fresh, creative ideas pop into your head when you're least expecting them. No wonder millions of runners consider their workouts the perfect time to reenergize both their bodies and their minds.

The Greeks had it right, of course. They understood the importance of the mind/body connection. Unfortunately, in this digital age, most of us have forgotten what the Greeks taught us.

I've read that we'll soon have wearable computers that are stitched into our clothing. These computers will go everywhere with us. We already carry portable cell phones, the better to keep in touch with the world at all times.

But what will we do, I wonder, to keep in touch with ourselves? For me, the answer is that I run. Because it keeps me fully tuned, both physically and mentally.

lesson two

Starting Lines

A starting line is the best, most exciting place I can imagine. When I stand on one, I feel fully alive—scared, yes, but also energized, focused, and prepared for the big challenge ahead. My head buzzes, my stomach grumbles, my feet twitch. My entire self—mind and body—is fully engaged. I can't wait to get going.

And I'm not talking only about the starting lines at running races. I'm talking about all beginnings. I'm talking about your first French class, your first day in college, your first day in a new relationship, your first day as a parent, your first day as an entrepreneur. And, yes, your first marathon. There's nothing like the thrill of the first time.

When I think back over my own life, with its full share of first days, I recall that they all terrified me. I didn't always go willingly. And yet I wouldn't have given up those days for anything. They were some of the best days of my life.

Beginnings are like that—both frightening and rewarding. Because of the fear factor, too many people shy away. They never take the steps forward that they should. They hesitate; they fumble about; they procrastinate; they count all the things that could go wrong.

Psychologists recognize this nearly universal tendency and have given it a name: catastrophizing. Faced with the need to imagine what might happen in new situations, many of us get caught up in the bad stuff. We see mainly darkness, not light. We get frozen in place; we don't get ourselves to the starting line.

Running has taught me, perhaps more than anything else, that there's no reason to fear starting lines . . . or other new beginnings. Over the years, I've gone out on tens of thousands of runs and entered thousands of races. Many of them have turned out badly. I've broken a bone in my foot, been attacked by a family of angry crows, been chased by snarling dogs, and nearly been struck by lightning.

Believe me, I could go on and on. I've had to hitchhike home on days when I couldn't complete a simple 5-mile workout, and I've dropped out of dozens of races, unable to reach the finish line.

All in all, I've had plenty of reasons never to run again. But I've kept at it because I've learned that these disappointments fade fast and aren't nearly as bad as they seem at first. The Finns, I've recently been told, have an expression that neatly drives home this point. It goes something like this: "Whatever you're imagining won't turn out nearly so bad."

When I first began running as a child, I had nothing to worry about. It was pure fun: those summer evenings, racing around barefoot in the backyard, playing tag or catching fireflies until

Mom came out with a glass of lemonade and a reminder that it was almost time for bed.

By high school, things had already grown more complex. I was playing on the jayvee basketball team . . . sort of. Actually, I was the worst player on the team, so I didn't get to play much. Coach Portelance put me in a game only once or twice and always when we were losing by 37 points with just 21 seconds to go.

But my teammates weren't much better than me. We lost most of our games, and it wasn't unusual for Coach to get frustrated over our ineptness. One day at practice, he simply threw up his hands in despair and hollered, "You guys aren't accomplishing anything on the court today. Get out there and run the cross-country course."

We all groaned. It was hard to imagine anything worse than being forced to run the hilly 3-mile cross-country course behind the high school.

But something totally unexpected—and in fact, life-changing—happened for me shortly after we began running. That's the beauty of starting lines: Until you begin a new venture, you never know what awaits you.

A mile or so into the cross-country course, it became clear that I was a better distance runner than anyone else on the basketball team. I left the others far behind. They were far better jumpers and dribblers and shooters than me in the gym, but here I had found my niche.

From that moment on, my life took a new direction. The next year, I tried out for the track and cross-country teams rather than basketball. From there, it was a straight line to a Boston Marathon victory and later to a great job at *Runner's World* magazine. Running has introduced me to hundreds of my best friends and given me opportunities I never dreamed about in my childhood.

My life is no more charmed than anyone else's. You name it—death, divorce, moving to a different part of the country. I've had to cope with life's brutal challenges, just like every single adult must do.

I've managed by convincing myself that new beginnings—starting lines—are my friend. This confidence comes, of course, from my experiences in running. On the starting line, I calm myself, I breathe deeply and slowly, I tell myself that I can get through this . . . and then I am ready.

Nothing ventured, nothing gained. That's the familiar old saw. I expand on it: Nothing started, nothing experienced, nothing learned, nothing finished.

Starting lines are one of the most important stations in life. We need to do more than just avoid them. We need to actively seek them out. Otherwise, we grow stagnant. We will disappear into black holes.

When you see the first hazy edges of a starting line begin to form in your life, don't avoid it. Don't look the other way. Try to bring the starting line into sharper focus. Consider its potential. Remember that if you don't go to the starting line, you will never view the whole course with all its possibilities.

And you will certainly never see the glories of the finish line.

THE ESSENTIAL TRAITS
OF A RUNNER

Every runner has unique traits, rituals, quirks, and passions. But these five traits are the ones that the most respected runners all share.

PATIENCE

I've never known a runner who had as much patience as he needed, but any and all amounts of this precious quality are invaluable. We runners simply don't get better fast enough to satisfy ourselves. Like the hare, we blast away from the starting line with visions of glory. We should be more tortoiselike. For that's the path to success.

Every runner gets injured at some time (always the wrong time). Every runner catches a cold or flu just before a big race. Every runner has to deal with marriage squabbles, job pressures, schoolwork, too much travel, or something related to these issues. When the frustrations and obstacles seem too great, every runner is tempted to quit.

This is when you most need patience. This is when you need to tell yourself that tomorrow or next week or next year is soon enough. Distance running requires you to take the long view. It takes weeks and months, at the least, to get in shape. Give yourself time. Don't make hasty and unnecessary mistakes. Remember: You're in it for the long run. Life is a marathon, not a sprint; pace yourself accordingly.

BALANCE

I admit to a fondness for obsessive people. I think they're often the very folks who achieve remarkable feats, and I was certainly quite obsessive when I won the Boston Marathon. But to achieve a deep, long-term contentment, it makes much more sense to find your balance point.

In running, as in life, moderation truly is the key. Marathons are great, particularly if you run one or two a year. Just enough to keep you in good shape through all four seasons. On the other hand, to run 52 marathons a year, which some people have done, seems ridiculous. What's the point? I used to feel compelled to run 14 times a week—twice every day. Now I run three or four times a week, do other cross-training, and enjoy it more than ever before.

If you're having fun, you've probably achieved balance.

The Essential Traits of a Runner

At times, you'll have fun by pushing yourself to achieve the most you can do. At many other times, however, you'll be satisfied by doing a little, not a lot, and keeping things in their proper perspective.

STOTANISM

This is a word that not many people recognize. In fact, it might not be a word at all, but it's definitely a great quality to have. The portmanteau word *Stotan* (or *Stotanism*) was coined by Percy Cerutty, the great Australian coach who led Herb Elliott to the gold medal and a brilliant world record for 1500 meters (the metric mile) in the 1960 Summer Olympic Games in Rome. Cerutty meant his new word to combine two others, *stoic* and *spartan*.

Stotanism is about toughness, though it doesn't imply an insensitive, superman approach. The stotan must be willing to stand on his own, to resist pain, to stick to his ideals. A stotan is quietly self-sufficient. He accepts the challenges of training, injuries, races, and disappointments without complaining, because he understands that simply by keeping on, by sticking to the path he has chosen, he will get stronger and better.

RESPECT

You can't go far in running without respect. First, you have to respect the distance, which is often said about marathons but applies equally to all distance running. If you don't understand the many ways running can challenge your body and mind, it can overwhelm you.

Second, there's the mutual respect all runners feel for each other. It doesn't matter what your 10-K time is or how fast I've run the marathon. The experience is what matters, and the experience is basically the same for all of us. An exercise physiologist can essentially "prove" that a 4-hour marathoner "works harder" than a 2-hour marathoner, even though it seems ludicrous to say this about the slower runner. But when different runners begin talking about a marathon, or any other running, they realize they've been through essentially the same thing. A true runner understands this.

HUMILITY

This is one of the surest lessons that running inevitably teaches. No one escapes unscathed. If you run, you will eventually face a disastrous day. You'll drop out of a race. You'll finish last. You'll finish first and say something stupid to a newspaper reporter. You'll trip and fall over a sidewalk crack. You'll run into a parked car while looking over the other shoulder.

And these are only the most commonplace things that will happen to you. Every runner invents ever more embarrassing ways to humiliate himself. Fortunately, humility is a positive force. It teaches you that, even after a stumble, you can get up and start running again. If you're lucky, maybe no one noticed. If they did, so what? Everyone stumbles at one time or another. It's the human condition.

lesson three

Connections

ON TAPPING THE PROFOUND
POWER OF HUMAN INTERACTION

We are standing backstage in the theater at St. George Community College in St. George, Utah. "We," in this case, means me and nine other members of the *Runner's World* magazine editorial staff. We have traveled here for the St. George Marathon, where, for the first time, we will lead marathon pacing teams. We don't know what to expect. Since we have never done this before, we aren't sure if the runners of the world will accept the pacing concept.

I had devised it several months earlier. The idea was simplicity itself. The marathon is a long and difficult challenge, and many runners go it alone. Even in fields of 10,000 to 20,000 participants, most have arrived by themselves from some other town or city. Few of the runners know anyone else in the huge throng. Even fewer know someone else who plans to run at their same pace.

But among the tens of thousands, surely there are hundreds who do, in fact, plan to run for a 3:00-hour goal—or 3:30 or 4:00 or 5:00. Why couldn't these runners be organized so that all would benefit from the spirit, sharing, and encouragement of a group effort?

That's what we hoped to do with the pacing team. A different *Runner's World* editor would lead each group. It sounded good in principle. The principle, however, hadn't been tested yet, and we didn't know if it would work.

Running has long suffered, in my opinion, from an early attitude best described and captured by the classic novella and movie of the same name: *The Loneliness of the Long-Distance Runner*. This is a story about rugged individualism, a long-standing American ethic (even though the author and setting are actually British). The hero, a prison inmate, refuses to accept the conditions and expectations of prison life, particularly of the warden. He runs to express his defiance, his uniqueness, his freedom. He may be a prisoner, he seems to be saying, but his soul cannot be contained.

Enough already. Maybe a prisoner needs to express his individuality, but most of us want to become a part of extended communities. We're looking for connections, not isolation.

I walk out onto the stage in St. George, but I can't see much, with the bright theater lights shining in my eyes. "Welcome to the *Runner's World* Pacing Teams," I say. "We're going to the Boston Marathon next April, and we want you to go with us." I have barely finished speaking when a roar envelopes me like the thunder of a dozen jets passing overhead. These people are ready to rock and roll.

The next day, the pacing teams helped literally hundreds of runners to accomplish their marathon goals, and we have continued leading other pacing teams at other marathons around the country. Everywhere we go, runners are eager to join a group, to have some fun, and to chase after their dreams.

We live in a world that is increasingly "connected," but sometimes I wonder. In my own office and in every other, I'm sure, we now send e-mail to our coworkers rather than walking 10 feet to talk to them. We look for Internet message boards and sign up for e-mails from groups that interest us. Digital wizards claim this gives us an increased sense of "community."

Again, I wonder about this kind of community. It's probably better than nothing, but does it build our humanity in a healthful way? Does it work if it becomes a substitute for real sharing and caring with other people?

Or does it simply increase the frequency of our communications with other people, while reducing the quality? Computers and cell phones are great for making contact with others. But they tend to make this contact a transaction rather than a sharing.

Talking directly and face-to-face with someone else adds so much. When we're together with others, be it one person or a group, our ears capture the spoken words, but our other senses pick up dozens of additional cues. Smiles and frowns, tears and tics, gestures and more subtle body language. These contribute greatly to the empathy that's at the heart of real communication. We're not just conducting transactions, we're talking with another person. A whole person.

As I write this chapter, the newspapers are full of stories about e-commerce. Soon, it appears, we'll be able to buy just about anything over the Internet, and we probably will. These purchases are always referred to as transactions. The Internet is only about 4 years old as a mass media, and already it has changed from a place known for building communities (this is what the newspaper stories were about just 2 years ago) to a place known for conducting transactions.

But I don't need more transactions in my life. I need more people. And running is one of the best

ways for me to find them. We all have certain
affinity groups, whether we're artists or architects or
anchovy fishermen. We tend to seek out others with
similar interests.

One of my big affinity groups is runners, and
running together turns out to be the best way to
share our passion. When I run with someone else,
the conversation flows naturally because . . . what
else can we do? We lift our knees to move forward,
and open our mouths to breathe more deeply. First,
to capture as much oxygen as possible. And second,
as a by-product, to talk.

Running removes us briefly from the fragmen-
tation and depersonalization of the digital world. It
gets us away from everything else: the phone, the
computer, the fax machine. Alone at last, we resort
to our oldest technologies—listening and talking.

Running seems to break down barriers. When
we run, we are already so exposed, often nearly
naked in our shorts and T-shirts, huffing and
puffing, purified by the effort. Briefly removed from
the defenses and secrets we maintain in so much of

our lives, we feel less need to hide our private thoughts, loves, fears, and stresses. We share. And our sharing begets more sharing in return.

I have fallen in love while running. I have learned about a friend's impending divorce and a colleague's heartbreaking miscarriage. A year later, on another run, she told me she was pregnant again, and everything was looking good. It stayed that way. Six months later, she had a darling little daughter.

Most running, even as practiced by Olympic champions, is not hard, fast, exhaustive running. It's relaxed and contemplative or conversational. Even the champions are advised by coaches and physiologists to run "easy" 80 percent of the time. The rest of us run easy anywhere from 95 to 99 percent of the time.

Beginning runners often ask how they can tell if they're running at the correct, easy level. The answer hasn't changed in the more than 3 decades that I've been running. There's a test for it. We call it the talk test. If you can run and carry on a normal conversation at the same time, you're running at the right pace. If you are huffing and puffing and have to pause between words, you're running too fast.

Slow down, enjoy the scenery, and ask your running buddies how they're doing. An easy training run provides the perfect opportunity for this. As more and more women have begun running, it has also become a great time for couples. Our busy days often don't provide enough chances for catching up on things. A run does.

We should throw out our watches when we run and count words instead. The more words exchanged, the better. Let the simple effort loosen your lips as well as your limbs. You don't need more electricity or battery power to get better connected. It's the opposite. Let human connection provide you with the electricity you need to be happy.

Winning

IN THE RACE TO BE YOUR BEST, THERE IS NO LOSING

The biggest road race I know, the San Francisco Bay to Breakers race, attracts about 75,000 runners every year. From that huge throng, one of them is first to cross the finish line. That one runner receives the first-place check and the next day gets to read his name in the newspaper headlines. The undeniable winner.

So what does that make the other 74,999 runners? Losers? Not in my mind. Not to all those runners.

One of the great benefits of running is that it teaches us to value the individual—*our self*. We may run a race with 75,000 others, but we're primarily concerned about our own outcome. The rest of the runners simply provide the backdrop for our own efforts. In truth, we don't care much about the winner's effort. We care only about our own.

Because we, too, want to "win" the race. And we can. We will. As long as we run a race that satisfies our own souls.

George Sheehan may have been the most competitive runner I ever knew. Widely known for his books and his more than 20 years of monthly columns in *Runner's World* magazine, Sheehan was acknowledged to be running's philosopher extraordinaire. His writings regularly quoted from the great thinkers—Voltaire to Emerson to William James—and attracted a wide audience.

But Sheehan's philosophical leanings never fooled anyone who knew him well and raced against him. Sheehan was first and foremost an elite athlete who ran so hard that he collapsed at the end of most road races. In fact, he seemed to measure his life by his race times and places. He was constantly comparing himself to other fast runners and their records.

Until he got cancer. The disease slowed him drastically, and Sheehan had to learn a whole new way to live. He was no longer winning races in his age division; he could no longer perform the way he had for decades. This was a shock. It forced him to see his life in many new ways.

In his final months, I kept trying to get Sheehan to come to my office for what I was calling "the last interview." Sheehan was an M.D., and he knew that he was dying—indeed, he was turning it into a book—and I felt that it was okay to talk to him about his impending end. More than that, I had to begin thinking about his obituary in *Runner's World*. He had been such a big part of the magazine for so long that I knew our readers would expect a full tribute after his death.

At first, Sheehan resisted the interview, but eventually, I prevailed. One summer day, his son George Jr. drove Sheehan to our offices. The so-often-triumphant runner was weak and pale, ravaged by cancer. He could walk only with his son's assistance. In 4 months, he would be gone.

Sheehan and I retreated to a quiet conference room, and I turned on the tape recorder. At first, he seemed hesitant. He started several answers slowly, almost gruffly. But then he would hit his stride and launch himself into a fascinating exploration. I was mesmerized. I felt privileged to have this time with him.

From the very first moment, I had known where the interview would end. I saved the biggest, most far-reaching question for last. "What's the single most important thing running has taught you about life?" I asked the running philosopher.

He began by explaining, as I knew, that he had always been a very competitive racer. He took great pride in his ability and his success. He ran to beat others. He would spot them warming up before the race and concentrate on beating them during the race. That all changed with the cancer.

"The most important thing I learned," he said,

"is that there is only one runner in this race, and that is me."

So too for the rest of us. We may enter races with 75,000 other runners in them, we may chart our times, we may line up our trophies on the mantelpiece, we may hope to see our names in the newspapers, but these are ultimately superficial. No one wins every race or forever. Everyone slows down. Everyone becomes reduced by the ravages of time, the side effects of a life fully lived.

Winning is not about headlines and hardware. It's only about attitude. A winner is a person who goes out today and every day and attempts to be the best runner and best person he can be. Winning has nothing to do with racing. Most days don't have races anyway. Winning is about struggle and effort and optimism, and never, ever, ever giving up.

Winning isn't about today, it's about tomorrow. A winner never rests on his laurels. It's not good enough to win one race or to have one good season. The winner is the person who gets up tomorrow morning and starts all over again, concentrating again on doing his best, whatever that might be.

I was fortunate enough, at one time in my life, to win a lot of races. One day, I even won a race the world considers important—the Boston Marathon. Believe me, I have cherished that day ever since. The Boston Marathon is a very special race, and anyone lucky enough to win it ought to understand that he has been blessed. I do.

But I also realize that it's just one race. It was many years ago. Few people, aside from me, remember that day. The year I won, 1968, was one of the most tumultuous in the American century, as it has been called. Martin Luther King was assassinated that year; Bobby Kennedy was assassinated that year. American cities burned while people rioted and protested. Against this backdrop, the 1968 Boston Marathon, and the gawky 21-year-old who won it, don't count for much.

This is fine with me because I'm much more concerned with today and tomorrow. What can I do right now to make myself a better, happier,

healthier person? What can I do to make a small difference in someone else's life?

We will all answer these questions in different
ways, but we must all share the same attitude: the
winner's attitude. We must realize that the quest
never ends. There is no finish line.

But we can make a difference. We can change
things for the better. We simply have to give our
best effort every day. If we are the best athlete and
best person we can be, then we have assuredly won
the race of life.

insight

A RUNNER'S HEROES

Here is an assortment of runners and nonrunners who have particularly inspired me over the past 4 decades.

JOHN A. KELLEY

I first met "Old John" A. Kelley when he was a young man of 60, still placing in the first half of many New England road races. Thirty years later, he was still going strong, having accumulated 59 Boston Marathon finishes—a record that may never be broken.

We runners naturally revere consistency, resilience, and great endurance, and Old John has more of these than anyone else I know. It comes, I believe, from an irrepressible spirit. These days, when he's not running and walking, Kelley spends his time painting and singing. His favorite song, which he offers whenever asked, is "Young at Heart." The man and the song couldn't be more perfectly matched.

ANNE FRANK

Most of my friends read Anne Frank's diary in high school, while I didn't encounter the sad but inspiring tale until my mid forties. Still, I can't imagine that the impact could have been any stronger. Here was a young woman living a nightmare—one that eventually claimed her life at 16. And yet she refused to give up or even alter her view of mankind. She wrote the wrenching, inspirational words: "In spite of everything, I still believe that people are really good at heart."

When we consider Anne Frank and her daily struggle to maintain good spirits, we realize the power of the human mind. It can deal with the worst disasters and turn them into shiny rays of renewed hope. The flu or a knee injury doesn't look so bad anymore; they will pass, and a brighter day will come.

CLARENCE DEMAR

DeMar won the Boston Marathon seven times, but running wasn't the only thing he did. He led a life marked by balance, community involvement, and a continuing quest for knowledge. After winning the 1911 Boston Marathon and participating in the 1912 Olympic Games, DeMar did not run marathons for a number of years because he felt his other obligations were more important. He taught Sunday school, worked at a fairly demanding job as a compositor, and took extension courses at Boston University and at Harvard. When he was ready to return to the Marathon in 1917, he finished third. He won the Boston Marathon again in 1922, 1923, 1924, 1927, 1928, and 1930. No one has ever come close to his record of seven Boston Marathon victories, and I don't believe anyone ever will.

ALBERT SCHWEITZER

I believe it was my German-born and music-loving mother who first introduced me to the life of Albert Schweitzer. Born in Upper Alsace, Germany (which is now part of France), in 1875, Schweitzer studied in both Berlin and Paris. At first, he concentrated on music, gaining fame as an organist. A few years later, he turned to theological writings, and then he began studying medicine.

As a medical missionary in Africa, Schweitzer found his life's work, his fame, and the basis for his 1952 Nobel Peace Prize. He treated the sickest of the sick, including lepers, and

built a hospital to provide permanent medical care. I was always impressed that a man who could have enjoyed a life of
luxury giving recitals to the rich and the royal instead found a
greater cause. He devoted his life to improving the health of
people who had nothing. Perhaps 15 years after I first heard
of Schweitzer, I entered the Peace Corps, hoping for a place-
ment in Africa. Instead, I was assigned to Latin America—a
different continent but one teeming with people in need.

ROBERTA GIBB

Bobbi Gibb was the flower child who ran for the joy of running. And when that joy led to the Boston Marathon, she
didn't stop. Okay, they wouldn't give her an official number.
So she crouched in the forsythia bushes near the Hopkinton
starting line, hopped into the race after it had begun, and
beat many of the men to Boston.

Later Gibb took up the law, and sculpture and environmental activism, approaching all these areas with the same
purity that she brought to running. And she still pops up in
Boston every couple of years to run the marathon again. You

can hardly miss her glowing, curly blond hair; the penetrating eyes; and the smile filled with a Zen-like contentment. She embodies the spirit of adventure and exploration that so many runners feel when they run.

KATHRINE SWITZER

Kathrine Switzer ran the Boston Marathon the year after Gibb did, only she had an official number on her shirt. This so enraged a Boston organizer, Jock Semple, that he tried to rip it off Switzer in full stride. He failed, but the photo of his ferocious charge and Switzer's recoiling fear will be remembered forever.

She could have been intimidated by this, but that wouldn't be Switzer. Not only did she finish the marathon, but she has also spent the rest of her life in tireless promotion of women's running. In the early 1980s, she led the successful fight to get the women's marathon into the Olympic Games. That was a tremendous success. Fifteen years later, Switzer began working again in running promotions, this time with the goal of helping average, non-Olympian women realize how running and other exercise can improve their lives. Always, she has seen and emphasized how fitness can bring more self-esteem and independence to a woman's life.

MARTIN LUTHER KING JR.

The great civil rights leader inspired everyone of my era. His cause seemed irrefutable; his words and person were larger than life. When he spoke, we listened. King, the Nobel Peace Prize winner in 1964, also had a contemplative side. If he had been a runner, which he wasn't, he would have used his daily exercise as a time-out for thought and problem solving.

King borrowed from other people and cultures—in particular, the pacifism that brought Gandhi success in India—and figured out how to meld the new notions with both African-American and Anglo cultures. He had to work with both, after all, to achieve his goal. I liked the way he built bridges to bring people together. I've always felt that we live happier, more successful lives when we reach out to others and involve them in our lives and our dreams.

JOHN J. KELLEY

I have mentioned "Young John" elsewhere in this book, but I can hardly leave him out of this section. When I was a high schooler first drawn to the mysteries and challenges of distance running, he was the mentor from whom I drew all knowledge.

Our coach-student relationship blossomed because it didn't come from him, the master. It came from me, the eager learner. He didn't need an ego boost; he didn't need to feed off my successes. He merely answered every question I asked. Lucky for me that he's a natural Irish raconteur. I spent untold hours in his kitchen drinking his wife Jessie's tea, enthralled by Kelley's tales. He was equally happy ruminating about marathon running, Jack Kerouac, organic gardening, Bob Dylan, environmental issues, or a dozen other topics. I can't imagine what my life would be like if I hadn't sat and listened to his monologues.

JOAN SAMUELSON

Samuelson, then Joan Benoit, did the impossible in 1984. No, I'm not talking about her victory in the first women's Olympic

Marathon. I'm talking about her win in the first U.S. women's Olympic Marathon Trials.

Seventeen days before that race, with her knee locked up in agonizing pain, she agreed to have arthroscopic knee surgery. There simply wasn't any alternative. And the minute she came out of surgery, she began to focus all her energies on the nearly impossible task in front of her—getting ready to run the most important marathon of her life. She got physical therapy, she spent hours every day with an ice pack on her knee, and she "trained" by lying on her back and pedaling a bicycle suspended from the ceiling.

And the mental work was harder. Samuelson had to erase all doubt from her mind. Otherwise, she had no chance. Sure enough, she won the Trials Marathon, the critical stepping-stone on her path to Olympic glory.

HELGA JOEL

My mother was born into an upper-middle-class Jewish family in Germany in 1920. As a teenager, she excelled at tennis, ranking among the top junior players in her country. But an ominous storm cloud—the rising tide of Hitler's power—soon put an end to her youthful sports career. Helga's father saw the writing on the wall earlier than most and arranged for his daughter to flee to Canada. There, she was "sponsored" by a university professor; otherwise, as an illegal immigrant, she would have been sent back home to Germany and almost-certain terror from the Nazis.

Eventually, she made her way to a U.S. college, where she played tennis on the men's team, and met and married my father. Mom was the most devoted, hardest-working person I've ever known, and the least-complaining, too. Living a less-privileged life than she had known as a child, she gave her all to her family—I remember the long hours in the kitchen, cooking, ironing, and working out long-division problems with me.

In midlife, she contracted stomach cancer and died in a local hospital. Tough to the end, she never acknowledged her disease to her three children, and we never had the chance to say a proper goodbye. That has pained us for decades, but we know we were blessed to have her as long as we did.

BILL RODGERS

Rodgers is one of the greatest long-distance runners of our times, clocking an astonishing 28 sub-2:15 marathons over a 9-year stretch in the 1970s and 1980s. We first met when we roomed together in college. It was the beginning of a friendship built on mutual respect that has lasted through the years. The two things I appreciate most about Rodgers are seemingly at odds with each other. The first is his incredible determination to excel—to be the best. I don't know any runner who "fights" harder than Rodgers in the heat of competition. The second quality is his humility. Rodgers looks and acts like the kid next door. He never asks for a special favor and is famous for sitting and signing autographs for hours after an exhaustive race. In running, Rodgers is the "People's Choice." His refreshing, easygoing manner have convinced many that running must be a great sport.

EMIL ZATOPEK

Zatopek, possibly the greatest runner of all time and a hero in his homeland, Czechoslovakia, protested the Communist invasion of 1968 and suffered many humiliating years when the totalitarians took over power in his country. Years earlier, he had won three gold medals—in the 5000 meters, 10,000 meters, and marathon—at the 1952 Olympic Games. He's still the only runner to have achieved this incredible "triple."

Zatopek was the hardest-training runner the sport has ever known, and the gentlest spirit. He loved to compete and then sit around and talk with his fellow athletes. He kept no secrets. When others wanted to know how he had enjoyed such great success, he willingly told them. He believed in freedom, sports, service, and a hearty laugh. His most touching gesture: Years later, he gave one of his gold medals to Ron Clarke, the courageous Australian distance star of the mid-1960s who never won an Olympic medal himself.

Traditions

THE NEED FOR ANCHORS
IN A FAST-RUNNING WORLD

As a teenager, I had already developed a jaundiced view of traditions. I guess the teen years are often filled with cynicism. I thought that some of my family's birthday traditions were contrived, not to mention Thanksgiving and Christmas and Easter and other holidays when we tended to do the same things in the same ways. And please don't even mention the annual vacation with Uncle Helmer.

To me, at that time, tradition meant the same old same old. Traditions were boring. They locked in the past without allowing a doorway to the future. I was young, and, of course, I wanted to do everything differently. I didn't need established frameworks; I saw them as prison walls. I wasn't yet wise enough to see how traditions make us stronger.

I craved adventure, which is why I got up early on Thanksgiving Day 1963 and drove to the Manchester Thanksgiving Day Road Race. It was the oldest road race in Connecticut, dating back to the 1920s, and it annually attracted more than 200 runners—200! an unimaginable number in 1963— not to mention tens of thousands of cheering spectators.

Most important of all, Manchester would be my first road race. I had been running on my high school track and cross-country teams for a little more than a year, and already I knew that my heart belonged to the roads. At last, I would no longer be confined to running endless laps on a 400-meter oval. On the roads, I could keep going as long as I wanted—for 5 miles, 10, 20, or the mystically appealing 26.2-mile marathon distance.

Manchester provided a raucous carnival atmosphere layered on top of a running race. As soon as I arrived, I saw people jogging up and down Main Street in turkey outfits. Others dressed as pumpkins and pilgrims. A band thumped out marching music, while a guy in a Scottish kilt played the bagpipes. It was easy to distinguish the fun-runners from the lean crew-cut superstar who had won the national collegiate cross-country championship several days before. I loved all the sights and sounds, and most of all, the energy that filled the air as I jogged around to warm up for the race.

Somehow, we all assembled on the starting line on time and got started. We pushed and shoved and leaned on each other to maintain our balance—many of us never having run with so many people at one time—but soon we were floating along smoothly, each on our own piece of the road.

Local residents lined the 5-mile course and cheered for us every step of the way. Some held up signs to encourage family members and friends, and the cheerleading squad from Manchester High was jumping and whooping for its favorites. I felt that I had never performed in front of such an enthusiastic and supportive crowd, and I'm sure all the other runners felt the same.

We finished with a long sprint down Main Street, where the crowds were four and five deep, leaning over each other on tiptoes to catch a glimpse of each runner as he ducked under the finish line. (Sorry, in 1963, every runner was a "he.") I think I finished 25th that day . . . or something like that. It wasn't important.

I'm pretty sure I won a trophy as the first high schooler to finish. Not important either. In the years to come, I would win Manchester nine times—a record that might take a few years for someone to break. Not important. (Because it will fall. I know that. All records fall.)

What's important then? Only that I loved the race, the experience, the adrenaline rush, the noise ringing in my ears, my heart practically bursting from the effort well and fully given. I couldn't wait to run Manchester again. By the time I graduated from college, I had finished Manchester 5 years in a row. A nice little streak.

I got married and continued running Manchester every Thanksgiving. I had children and continued running Manchester. I ran it in snow and rain and high winds.

I moved to another state and continued running Manchester. I got divorced and continued running Manchester. I ran at the front of the pack, in the middle, and at the back, hobbled one year by walking pneumonia, another year by an Achilles tendon injury, another by a busy work schedule that had precluded much training.

I didn't care where I finished. That no longer mattered. The only thing that counted was getting to Manchester and going the distance.

Thus are traditions born. I couldn't tell you when Manchester evolved for me, from something I did because I hoped to take home the first-place trophy to something I did because it had earned a major spot in my life. But the evolution *did* occur.

And it caused me to reevaluate many of the other traditions in my life. The ones that I had scorned many years earlier. The holidays and reunions. Now I began to see these transitions differently. In a world that perpetually moves faster, never slower, we need all the anchoring points we can find. Chaos erupts spontaneously in our spinning lives. It's the center of the wheel that we need to focus on more often.

According to one old saying, Familiarity breeds contempt. And it was something like that that once caused me to rail against traditions. Now, I see many reasons for revisiting the familiar.

Traditions, whether big and public or small and private, have a magical power. They give us strength and stability, while reconnecting us with the people and places we love.

Now, rather than avoiding traditions, I look everywhere for opportunities to start new ones. A particular favorite: Every summer I ask all the members of my family, from youngest to oldest, to gather for a swimming fest and group photo on a timeworn wooden dock where my sister, brother, and I swam as children.

And I continue running Manchester every Thanksgiving Day. At last count, I had run there 37 years in a row. I'm aiming for 50. More would be better.

Time

ON THE FUTILITY OF BEING
A MASTER OF MINUTES

I am running the greatest footrace on Earth—a race few Americans have ever heard of. It's called the Comrades Marathon, and it's held annually in South Africa. One of the many things that's different about Comrades is that it's much longer than the standard 26-mile marathon. It's more like a double marathon—54 miles of undulating hills between Pietermaritzburg and Durban.

Or Durban and Pietermaritzburg. Give those South Africans some credit for creativity. The Comrades Marathon changes direction every year. The odd-numbered years are "down" years, from P-burg to Durban. On even-numbered years, the course runs "up" from Durban to P-burg.

But I haven't yet mentioned what makes Comrades unique. In any other country, you might expect a dozen or two slightly daft runners to enter a hilly 54-miler. In South Africa, Comrades annually attracts 15,000 runners. The entire country practically shuts down to focus its attention on Comrades. The leading TV network provides 9 hours of uninterrupted live coverage.

Comrades has history, it has mass and spectacle, and I have been wanting to run it for 20 years. Now I am finally there, 15 miles into the race, and all those other runners are getting in my way. The road is packed with runners, shoulder to shoulder, and when we reach a hill, they all start walking.

I mean, all of them. What's wrong with these South Africans? I have a specific goal time in mind, and I can't stop myself from glancing anxiously at my watch whenever I bump into a wall of walking runners. Which is far too often. For a few miles, I bob and weave and push my way through any small cracks I find.

Then it hits me: This is a total waste of energy. I may save a second here and a second there, but I'm expending minutes' worth of effort in the process. Besides, many of these runners have completed five or six previous Comrades. Maybe they know something I don't know. It would make a lot more sense to slow down and go with the flow.

I give it a try, and it feels good, so I keep on in the same manner. When the pack runs, I run. When the packs slows to a walk, I walk. And it works. I finish strong, I still achieve my performance goal, and I enjoy myself all the way. Which is an important thing when you're running 54 miles.

The Comrades experience reinforces something I've been trying to learn all my life. I don't always need to be in a rush. I don't always need to be doing three things at once. I don't always need to feel that Father Time is closing in on me, and I'd better go faster if I want to stay ahead of him.

I got off to a bad start when I was in junior high school. One day in English class, we read the Rudyard Kipling poem "Time." The poem's most famous line stopped me cold. It seemed a life lesson, something I should adopt as my personal mantra. And I did. The words lodged in my brain, where they have remained ever since: "If you can fill the unforgiving minute/With sixty seconds' worth of distance run/Yours is the Earth and everything that's in it/And—which is more—you'll be a Man, my son!"

Being young and impressionable, I was looking for windmills to tilt at, and this poem provided all the challenge I needed. I had already started running. Soon I would be an aspiring high school and college star. The path to success seemed clear: I simply had to fill more minutes and hours with distance run. I quickly began the quest.

As it turned out, I was good at this, literally. I

could run miles and miles. I seemed to be suc-
ceeding. I was filling lots of minutes with lots of
miles. I recall, in particular, that I grew interested in
entering a special running race called the 1-hour
run. It's a race on a track that lasts for exactly 60
minutes. Whoever covers the most laps in 60 minutes wins the race.

In all other races, the finish line has a physical location, and you are always running toward
it. In a 1-hour run, there is no finish line. You
simply fill the hour with as much "distance run" as
you can.

One-hour runs were always hard to find, and
today they're practically extinct, but eventually, I lo-
cated one. In this race, the starter fired his pistol
twice—once at the beginning and once at the end,
after precisely 60 minutes had elapsed. The second
time we runners heard the pistol, we had to freeze
in our tracks until an official came out to measure
our spots on the track.

I remember the pride I felt at completing 48½
laps. That meant I had gone slightly more than 12

miles in an hour, averaging just under 5 minutes per mile for the duration.

Now the whole thing seems diabolical to me. I see the futility of it. Like the Red Queen in Lewis Carroll's *Through the Looking Glass*, I realize that "it takes all the running you can do to keep in the same place. If you want to get somewhere else, you must run at least twice as fast as that!"

"Distance run" is no longer important to me. Time, of course, is. It must be. Time is the very stuff of life, the most precious substance we have. In the literal sense, our time is limited—the length of our days, the length of our lives.

When something is this important, it shouldn't be hurried. It shouldn't be squeezed full of endless activities, running or otherwise. Now I try to slow down whenever I can. Not because I want to extend time and cram more miles into it, but because I want to enjoy my best moments.

I run more slowly; I don't measure my courses; I don't time how fast I'm going. A run is most meaningful and most enjoyable when it exists for its own sake, when it doesn't feel the pressure of a ticking stopwatch. The same goes for most other activities.

I've decided to forgive the unforgiving minute. It made me hurry about too much, but I've learned from my mistake. I don't do any filling anymore. I let the 60 seconds fill me. It's a much more energizing way to live.

THE MUSIC OF RUNNING

I do not favor wearing headphones while running—to me, the music gets in the way. But that doesn't mean running doesn't produce memorable rhythms and stimulating sounds. It does. Here are a few of my favorites.

THE BELL LAP

In all track races longer than one lap, the finish-line officials ring a bell to signify that just 1 lap remains. In the 800-meter race, the runners have completed only 1 previous lap; in the 10,000, they have completed 24 laps before they hear the sweet peal of the bell. The bell strikes for a freedom of sorts, because now the race is nearly done. The runners can throw off their fears and sprint with wild abandon, no longer concerned about pacing themselves and jockeying for position. Everything else has been a prelude. This at last is climax. The bell signifies that the race has reached its crescendo; the runners have pushed as long and as hard as they can push. Now the true champions will emerge.

"BORN TO RUN"
BY BRUCE SPRINGSTEEN

The influence of rock-and-roll music was so pervasive in the second half of the twentieth century, and its rhythms so driving and energetic, that every runner has a favorite rock anthem. Or a dozen of them. Mine is the Springsteen classic. To get motivated for a workout, I only need to hear the opening bars of music and the words, "In the day we sweat it out on the streets . . ." I can be down, depressed, and depleted, and this music will still pump me up. I especially like playing it in the car when I'm driving to a race; for me, it's the perfect psych-up song.

BAGPIPES

The bagpipe was designed to be played outdoors and is part of the oldest continuously contested track meet, the Braemar Games of Scotland. My personal favorite road race, the Thanksgiving Day Manchester Road Race in Connecticut, somehow manages to position a bagpipe player every year at the top of the course's steepest hill. His loud, piercing music sounds like the rasp of my breathing, like my lungs' desperate search for air. There's something about the bagpipe's mournful sound that gives us strength when we run, for in its presence, we feel that we are not alone. We feel that someone or something else understands our suffering.

STARTER'S GUN, CROSS-COUNTRY RACE, CRISP FALL MORNING

Cross-country was the earliest form of distance running and remains the most pristine, a race of athletes against the environment—often a twisting, hilly, even muddy environment. On a late October morning, a frost may cover the grass, so the runners make a crunching sound as they go through their warmup paces. Soon, they are ready to begin, bent motionless over the starting line, blowing puffs of white air, waiting, waiting, waiting. The silence grows deafening, but then the starter's finger presses against the trigger; a shot rings out. Stillness turns to movement; quiet, to the scuffling sound of a hundred frantic legs. And

the race is underway, the oldest and simplest sport reen-
acted again, much as it has been for a millennium or more.

"CHARIOTS OF FIRE" BY VANGELIS

For the last 2 decades, many road races have used their
starting-line amplifiers and speaker systems to play either the
theme from *Rocky* or the theme from *Chariots of Fire* to get
runners in the mood for racing. I like them both, I have to
admit, but *Chariots* is my favorite of the two. I recall the movie
of the same name, of course, with its twin themes of pursuing
a goal and remaining true to one's faith, and particularly the
opening scene where the young British Olympians splash
across a beach to the rousing synthesizer music by Vangelis.
No words. But somehow you can clearly hear the heartbeats
pounding, and it always makes mine do the same.

FIRST AVENUE, NEW YORK CITY MARATHON

Simon and Garfunkel called it the 59th Street Bridge. Feelin'
groovy. Others know it as the Queensboro Bridge at the 15-

mile mark of the New York City Marathon. Feelin' pretty darn tired. But then, a miracle. As the runners trudge down off the bridge, they make a looping 270-degree turn that takes them back under the bridge and deposits them on Manhattan's First Avenue. They pass from darkness into light, from relative quiet into a thunderclap of applause. On lower First Avenue, the crowds are five and six deep; they are hanging from apartment windows; they are dancing on rooftops and celebrating their favorite day of the year—Marathon Day. And all of them are screaming, yelling, and beating drums for the runners. This ain't Broadway, but for a runner, it's as good as it gets. And I've never met a runner who didn't appreciate the limelight and the recognition.

Listening

A light snow has been falling for an hour, an inch already covers the roads. It's nighttime, a little past 9:00 on a mid-December evening, and I'm out running about town. I turn down the side streets, the back alleys. This is my favorite time for a quiet run.

There are no cars on the street, no wind rattling through the bare tree branches. The snow falls straight down, the big five-sided flakes dropping so slowly that I can spot one in mid-descent, run toward it, and stick out my tongue to catch it. A snow-sickle. I've never tasted anything as pure and coolly refreshing.

The night is so perfectly calm that I hear only two sounds. One is the light "crunch-crunch" of my shoes on the inch of snow. We runners love this cushiony compacting, so much softer and more comfortable than the usual slapping of our shoes on hard asphalt and concrete. The crunchy snow sounds like a lullaby and has the same effect: It induces a near-dreamlike euphoria.

It's the other sound that keeps me from falling asleep—the sound of mindless thoughts flitting through my head. I have heard a million people say that running is the most boring activity that they can possibly imagine. Since I'm sure I'm not any smarter or wittier than these people, I can only guess that they never learned to listen as they run. If they did, they would surely be entertained and informed by their own thoughts.

Sometimes my main reason for running is simply to see where my brain will go while my body is meandering through the local trails or roadways. It can never be predicted, and it's always a surprise. Since I'm a runner, I often find myself

musing on future workouts or races, flashing forward to mull over the races I'd like to enter next
year or the year after.

Since I'm a writer and editor by profession, I
more often find that my mind chooses to deal
with the problems of the day. I'm hardly alone in
this. A week before I sat down to write this
chapter, *The New York Times* published an essay by
the prolific author Joyce Carol Oates. In the *Times*,
she said, "Running! If there's any activity happier,
more exhilarating, more nourishing to the imagi-
nation, I can't think what it might be. In running
the mind flees with the body; the mysterious ef-
florescence of language seems to pulse in the
brain, in rhythm with our feet and the swinging of
our arms."

When I run, I'll often work out several story
ideas for an upcoming issue of *Runner's World* magazine. Or figure out how to reorganize a story that's
sitting on my desk, waiting to be edited. Without
fail, I think about stories I'd like to write myself
when I get the chance.

Sometimes, I simply work on sentences. You have to be a writer, I suppose, to appreciate the subtleties of the sentence. It can be long or short, simple or complex, direct or inverted. When I am running, I enter an almost-subconscious state where the words of a sentence begin arranging themselves in my head. And when they settle into a particularly elegant design, being a writer, I experience a tingle of satisfaction. The workout has rewarded me with a small but pleasing gift. I return with something I didn't have when I started.

This wouldn't happen if I weren't listening to myself. It wouldn't happen if I were dodging traffic in a busy city. It wouldn't happen if I were wearing headphones.

I have tried without success to understand why so many runners wear headphones. The safety factor is a big deterrent, of course. If you're wearing them, you're less likely to hear the car spinning out of control behind you. You won't be ready to make the small jump to the shoulder of the road that could save your life. You won't hear someone sneaking up from behind either.

But I have an even larger issue with headphones. I can't imagine someone not listening to the world around them—the birds, the rainfall, their friends, the crunch of running shoes on new-fallen snow. Or simply their own thoughts. The ability to listen, in all its forms, seems to me one of our most-human gifts. We cannot learn without listening; we cannot empathize without listening; we cannot make good decisions without listening to both heart and mind.

I am intrigued by the relationship between listening and decision making. Being part of the corporate management world, I am frequently sent to seminars designed to make me a better listener. Here, we learn how to encourage and receive feedback from all the people we work with. The seminars are often worthwhile, and I always try to use some of the principles that are taught.

The more meetings I attend, however, the more I believe that something crucial is being left out. Yes, it's important to listen to everyone around you. But it's even more important to learn how to listen to yourself. Whether a decision is purely personal or involves dozens or even hundreds of others, *you alone* are the person who has to make it, and you can only do it after listening to your own internal monologue.

Through countless hours of practice, running has taught me to listen to myself and to believe in my decisions. I have made decisions as small as a magazine cover selection and as big as a divorce or the firing of the person who worked most closely with me. I have learned that there's no such thing as an easy decision. But I have also learned that it's much better to make decisions and move on than to be trapped in the agony of the process.

Running, of course, teaches us to move on. There is always another day, another workout, another mile, another race. But more important, it teaches us to listen to ourselves and believe in ourselves.

How strange that running, which seems so outwardly physical, is actually the most thought-full of activities. If you slow down and pay attention, you will be amazed at what you hear. And you will find that the thoughts that surface during a workout run strong and true through all the parts of your life.

Losing

WHY ALL PATHS, INCLUDING FAILURE, ULTIMATELY LEAD TO VICTORY

Losing is such a universal experience that you'd think we would all become experts at it. That we'd develop a thick skin, that we'd learn to bounce back quickly, that we'd realize that we need a new vocabulary. "Losing" just doesn't work. It sounds so terminal.

Unfortunately, most of us don't become experts at it. We equate losing with failure, and we let ourselves be defeated. Instead of becoming experts who bounce back, we become victims who don't try again. I've had my share of losses, but I refuse to become a victim. Instead of viewing my losing efforts as dead ends, I turn them into detours, and I keep moving forward.

In running, I twice lost in the biggest race I ever attempted: the U.S. Olympic Marathon Trials. Like any accomplished athlete, I set the Olympics as my greatest goal. I wanted it more than anything. Twice I ran in the Olympic Trials, hoping to make the U.S. Olympic Team, and twice I fell short.

I had imagined that these losses would prove devastating. In both cases, however, I soon found myself on a different and unexpectedly rewarding path.

Nineteen-sixty-eight should have been my year for making the Olympic Team. I won the Boston Marathon in April, and the Olympic Trials were scheduled for mid-August, just days before my birthday. The stars were aligning for my big Olympic effort. At least that's what I tried to tell myself every morning when I got up for my 10-mile workout.

Unfortunately, I pulled a leg muscle about a month after winning Boston, and it didn't heal completely in time for the Trials. I started the race, but I couldn't complete it. In fact, I was standing by the finish line, already showered, as several friends ran down the final straightaway and claimed their spots in the Olympics. So much for my big dream.

After the unhappy Trials marathon, I had no reason to do any running. I spent the last 2 weeks of that summer hanging out at the beach. As a result, by September 1, my leg was totally healed. When I received an invitation to run an international race in Canada, I decided to accept. Three weeks later, I won that race with one of the best performances of my career.

This gave me pause. I asked myself: What had I learned from the Olympic Trials? For one thing, that you can never expect a muscle or other injury to heal on your schedule. Heal it will, but on its own timetable.

More important, I learned that losing isn't contagious. It's not a fatal condition, and it's not forever. It's more like a cold that makes you miserable for a week but then goes away, and you're fine.

Eight years later, I was ready for another shot at the Olympics. Again, the signs were good. I had been training and racing well for several years; I had a steady job; my personal life was stable. And this time I was completely healthy. I actually finished the race.

In fact, I had one crystalline moment when I thought my Olympic dream was going to come true. I remember it so clearly. Just past the 10-mile mark, the course made a couple of zigzag turns and then emptied onto a long, straight avenue. I was running in a pack of five and happened to be the first through the several turns.

Ahead of us, I saw Frank Shorter and Bill Rodgers, two runners we all expected to finish one-two, which they did. That left one spot open for another runner to make the team.

I also saw two other runners ahead of me, both athletes I knew well and felt confident of catching and passing. That left me in, gulp, third place—the magic position. The thought struck with such impact that I can recall it decades later as if it were a mere 5 minutes ago: "Ohmigoodness, you could be going to the Olympics."

Well, not quite. I did catch and pass the two runners ahead of me, and I poured every ounce of myself into the quest to finish third. But I made one serious miscalculation. In my eagerness for third place, I struck too soon. I got there, but I couldn't hold it. Several other runners, more patient than I, conserved their energy for the crucial last 6 miles. They steamed past me at the 22-mile mark.

Fatigued and depressed, I faded to 10th place. Not a bad effort—and I certainly believed that I had given it my all—but not good enough to make the team. In the harsh arena of the Olympic Trials, I had once again failed to measure up. What next?

I was 30 now, and I had other interests that I could pursue. But first I had to deal with my marathon career. I had given a solid decade of my life to making the Olympic Team, and so far I hadn't made the mark.

I could continue, of course. I could look at the foundation I had constructed—the tens of thousands of training miles—and try to find a way to make it even stronger and higher. The Olympics would come around again in another 4 years. Maybe that would be my time.

Or I could move on. I could acknowledge that I would have to go through life without achieving my greatest dream—the Olympics. There would be no storybook ending.

The answer didn't come to me from endless soul-searching. There was no mental agony. The answer came, as it should have, from the running itself.

I no longer had the spark. It was that simple. I didn't have the energy for it any longer. It was too hard to kick-start myself in the mornings. My body said, "No more." It was obviously time to move on.

I was fearful at first. I worried that letting go of one goal, the Olympics, would set a precedent that would follow me the rest of my days. A failure. I didn't like the sound of that word.

So I didn't accept it. Okay, I hadn't made the Olympic Team, but surely I could find other challenges. My life didn't end. I simply swung wide around the roadblock and set off on a new course, one that soon led to many entrancing vistas. I explored many of them, trying new things, and quickly discovered that my 10-year Olympic quest hadn't taught me failure. Indeed, the discipline and training and goal setting had prepared me for success in other areas.

I kept running, but without expectations and pressures. It became simply a process-path to good health, stress relief, creative thinking, and fun times with friends. More than 20 years later, I can honestly say that running this way is far more enjoyable than striving for the Olympics.

I have learned that there is no failure in running, or in life, as long as you keep moving. It's not about speed and gold medals. It's about refusing to be stopped. You might find that one particular direction proves difficult, but there are many directions on a compass. Infinite, in fact. As long as you keep searching, you'll find your winning way.

THE TRANSCENDENT MOMENTS OF A RUNNER

What are the most precious, most emotional moments in running? Here are my six favorite.

RUNNING AT SUNRISE

For reasons that I can't begin to explain, any day will be better if you start it off with a run. And not just any run. It has to be a run that begins before sunrise and welcomes the day's first light.

Let me confess: I don't do this often—perhaps a half-dozen times a year, and usually during the summer when vacationing at the shore. On those occasions, I can run facing eastward and watch the sun rise over the water's edge. This simple act—my own movement, coupled with the sun's gradual movement up from the horizon—fills me with joy and hope. I always stop to catch my breath for a moment and to marvel at the miracle of a new day. Then I am off running again, fully renewed.

THE FIRST RACE

Whether I'm traveling around the country giving clinics or sitting in my office answering e-mails, here's one of the questions I get asked most often: "I think I'm ready to enter my first race, and I really want to do one, but I'm also really scared. I don't know anything about racing, and I'm afraid I'll finish last. What should I do?"

The people at Nike might say, "Just do it." And I don't think I can say it any better. There's such power in action, such excitement, such reward. All runners remember their first races with a rush that the years hardly diminish. The new sights and sounds, the incredible adrenaline buzz—there are as many different reasons to enter races as there are runners, but the most important one is "Because they're there and because you can never be a better athlete and person than you are during a race." You don't get that chance every day.

RUNNER'S HIGH— AND RUNNER'S "MELLOW"

A runner's high is a special experience that most runners don't have all the time (an important point) but do get at irregular, unpredictable intervals. So don't begin running because you expect every workout to be like some other kind of "high" you might have experienced. The true but rare runner's high is a zone that we enter when everything seems to click perfectly, when time stands still, and when we can run almost without effort.

This happens for me about once or twice a year. That's why I put more emphasis on the runner's "mellowness," which is simply the warm, contented feeling that almost all runners have after nearly every run. In fact, unless you get physically sick from something you've eaten, it's almost impossible to feel bad after running. This mellow happiness is one of the immediate rewards of running that keep many of us always looking forward to our next run.

CRESTING HEARTBREAK HILL

Because of the Boston Marathon's stiff qualifying standards, this is not something every runner can accomplish. Indeed, only about 5 to 10 percent of the overall marathoning population is fast enough to qualify for Boston. Nonetheless, Heartbreak Hill is so special that it makes all the training sacrifices more than worthwhile.

Heartbreak Hill sits at the 21-mile mark of the Boston Marathon, the last of four undulating hills in the town of Newton, Massachusetts. Standing alone, not far from the street where you live, Heartbreak Hill wouldn't amount to much. It only rises 100 feet or so. But at this late juncture in the Boston Marathon, it's sheer torture.

Fortunately, the crowds on Heartbreak Hill are the thickest and most voluble of any along the entire, spectator-lined course. You may want to give up and start walking, but they don't want you to. They won't let you. Slacken your pace just a smidgen, and they'll spot you, yelling, "Don't walk. You can do it. You're nearly at the top, and it's all downhill from there." True enough. Which, coupled with the crowd's cheering, is why you'll make it over Heartbreak Hill without walking.

RUNNING WITH A PARTNER

We runners have our friends and our training partners, and the best are the ones who are both. These are the ones we share our world with, whether scuffling down a busy suburban street or running quietly on the soft, moist trails of a northwestern forest.

I run with some of these friends on an almost-daily basis; others, every week or two; and still others, only once a year. Sometimes distance erects barriers. But distance and days apart fade rapidly after just 5 minutes of running together again. Once a running partner, always a running partner. We both talk excitedly. We catch up on all the important personal news. We barely notice as the minutes and miles melt away.

I love almost all my daily training runs. But the best by far are the ones when I'm running with a regular training partner. On these runs, I feel relaxed and connected, physical and human, a friend with a friend.

SLAPPING HANDS WITH KIDS AT THE SIDE OF THE ROAD

Any big race has thousands of spectators observing from the sides of the road, and among those thousands are always a fair share of kids—youngsters from age 6 to 10. Their parents tend to watch from a distance, perhaps applauding politely. The kids want more. They crowd as close to the road as they dare, and reach out an expectant hand.

When I was fast, I kept away from the kids. We competitive runners clung to the middle of the road. We had little concern or interest in things going on at our periphery. We only cared about staying close to the motorcycle escort in front of us and trying to beat each other. Our tunnel vision didn't extend to the sides of the road.

Nowadays, I don't worry about finishing first, and I don't worry much about beating other runners. There are no motorcycle escorts anywhere near me, so I look for other distractions. And it's those young and hopeful faces, those extended hands, that draw me in. When I see one, I zigzag to the side of the road and give it a loud slap. I feel that I am passing the torch in a way. But I also find that the effort gives me an extra burst of energy. Doing something with or for kids always makes me feel so much younger myself.

Materialism

WHAT YOU REALLY NEED,

YOU ALREADY HAVE

We runners are the luckiest of athletes. We don't need any special equipment or facilities or conditions to enjoy all the benefits of our sport. No clubs or gloves or racquets. No pools or courts or country clubs. We don't need to wait for a particular season—summer or winter—to go out and have a great workout.

Our running shoes are sitting there, in the closet or basement or garage, waiting for us. All we need do is lace them on, and open the door.

That's all it takes—a decent pair of running shoes. Or does it take even that? Charlie "Doc"

Robbins has been running road races without shoes for nearly 50 years; I've known him for the last 30, and I've learned many things from him that no one else has even considered. The most valuable: The equipment doesn't make the runner (or the person).

I first got to know Doc well in the mid-1960s, when I was a student at Wesleyan University in Middletown, Connecticut, and he was a psychiatrist at a nearby hospital. When the other doctors went out for their rounds of golf on Wednesday afternoons, Doc showed up at our Wesleyan track or cross-country practices.

We college runners would be wearing our shiny new warmup suits and the latest pair of running shoes. Doc, then in his early forties, would be in torn khakis, a World War II–surplus wool shirt, and his bare feet. The pants and shirt were enough to draw attention to him, but it was, of course, the lack of running shoes that made Doc famous.

He deserved to be famous, too. Several decades earlier, a pioneer among American distance runners, Doc had ranked among the very best in the country at distances from 5 miles to the marathon. He often placed in the top 10 at the Boston Marathon, and did even better at the in-between distances like 10 miles and 20 kilometers. In fact, he won numerous national championships at these distances.

Doc was a student of the sport, forced to analyze every minute and every mile, because his medical studies (first) and medical career (later) didn't allow him much time for training. He was also an iconoclast and experimenter. He tinkered with running more than anyone I have ever known, figuring out, among other things, how to do a great workout in just 10 minutes and how to run efficiently on both uphills and downhills (few runners excel at both).

At a time before we had terms like *ergonomics* and *efficiency expert*, Doc exemplified both. One of his conclusions: Running shoes were basically useless. He believed and practiced the art of running efficiently without shoes. (When the outside temperature dips below 40°F, Doc will often pull on a pair of socks, because the road gets harder and the feet more sensitive when it's cold. But that's as well-shod as he ever gets.)

Knowing that Doc was coming to practice, I looked forward to every Wednesday.

There was nothing better than an engaging workout with him. We took it easy—me in my warmup suit and fine shoes, him in his khaki pants and no shoes—and discussed everything there was to discuss about running.

As a college student at the time, I took classes all week long. But I considered this my only one at the Ph.D. level. None of my other teachers was as brilliant in his or her field as Doc, a true "roads scholar," was in his.

I even ran a few races barefoot, and did well in them, too. I can't claim, though, that I adopted Doc's always-shoeless approach. I only dared go barefoot on nicely trimmed golf courses and smooth, rubberized tracks. But not on the rough and unpredictable roads. On the roads, Doc was one of a kind.

More important, I adopted his the-shoes-don't-make-the-runner philosophy. And seeing how true this proved to be in running, I could more clearly see that it pertains to the rest of life as well.

I've known runners who believed that they would get faster if only they could find the perfect pair of shoes. The perfect fit, the perfect lightness, the perfect high-tech features. But I've never known a runner who actually improved after getting a new pair of shoes. Shoes can't make you faster. Only dedication, consistency, passion, and hard training can make you faster.

We search too much for false prophets. Some runners believe that they must move to a running mecca like Boulder, Colorado, or Eugene, Oregon. Other runners believe that they need a new coach. Still others believe that they need expensive heart-rate monitors or, perhaps, regular visits to an exercise physiology laboratory.

These runners believe, in other words, that they are most likely to find success by discovering new baubles in the physical world outside themselves. I disagree. I think these baubles are almost always false prophets. Success comes from within. It comes from consistent dedication to core principles and values.

I believe that we are all born with the tools we need to be the best we can be. Unfortunately, we live in a maddeningly materialistic world that tries to tell us the opposite. We are inundated with advertisements and testimonials designed to convince us that something else can make us better.

A new pair of running shoes can make us run faster. A new computer can make us smarter. A new car can make us more successful. A new food can make us thinner. A new fund can make us richer. A bigger house can make us more popular.

In fact, these are all empty promises. I've tried all of the above, and the claims have always proven false. Our culture bombards us with temptations, and it takes a strong person to resist the constant allure.

The answers lie within, not outside. The best solutions are achieved from personal resolve, not from multiple credit cards.

I still see Doc Robbins once a year at the annual Thanksgiving Day Race in Manchester, Connecticut. I have run it 37 years in a row. He has run
it 45 years in a row. I am still the student; he is still
the master.

He is also still running barefoot. Not only
that, but his khaki pants and wool shirt look suspi-
ciously like the ones I remember from our workouts
together at Wesleyan in the mid-1960s. The moment I first lay eyes on Doc each Thanksgiving
morning, I break into a big, spontaneous smile.

I can't help it. Shaking hands with Doc, I feel
once again the power of turning away from materialistic temptresses and concentrating on the essen-
tials. I already have everything I need to enjoy
happiness and success. I don't have to reach outward
to pluck anything else. I only have to look inward
and make good use of my personal resources.

Brothers

**IN THE LONG RUN,
THERE WILL ALWAYS BE FAMILY**

After winning the Boston Marathon in 1968, I developed the custom of returning to Boston and running the marathon again every 5th year. Now, on Patriots' Day 1998—30 years from the day that lifted my life—I am once again making the long run from Hopkinton to Boston. And things aren't going well at all.

I've covered only 6 miles, and already I feel tired and disgruntled. I need someone or something to lift my spirits.

At times like this, my family has always provided. When I was young, my father and grandfather attended all my races, often driving me hundreds of miles. My mother somehow dealt with the piles of sweaty laundry and the then-weird requests for foods like yogurt and wheat germ. My brother, Gary, occasionally ran with me, and my sister, Natalie (whose right leg is amputated below the knee), cheered equally for my best and most pitiful efforts.

I know it's a truism to praise family support, but that doesn't mean it should ever go unacknowledged. Besides, in my family it didn't come easily. We didn't fight, but we didn't talk either. We were a family of quiet, stoical doers—not one for big celebrations or loud chest-thumpings.

As I head toward the 7-mile mark in the 1998 Boston, I begin to look for Gary and my wife Cristina. They've promised to meet me there and at several other points along the course. When I spot a large neon sign that says, "Go Amby," I immediately recognize Cristina's artwork. A moment later, I pick out both their faces and hear their shouts of encouragement.

And then I am past them, once again fighting

my lonely battle against the 26.2-mile course. When I hear Gary's "How are you doing?" question linger in the air, I respond by putting my hand out, palm down, and giving it a wishy-washy flick at the wrist. Not so great.

In about 30 seconds, a runner catches me from behind and strides close to my side. It's Gary. He had always intended to run the last 10 miles with me, so he had dressed that morning in his running gear. Now he would have to go 19 miles—far more than planned. Far more than he was trained for. But he had felt my distress at a visceral level, and re-acted to it instantly. He knew I needed help.

As a high schooler, Gary had run faster times than I had achieved 3 years ahead of him. He was hotly recruited by a number of colleges, but pretty much gave up on running in college. He had other interests. Why not pursue them?

We drifted slowly apart. Our family—quiet, almost severe—hadn't prepared us for staying in close contact. But I always get a tear in my eye when he tells the story of that April afternoon in his freshman year. He cut classes, grabbed a cheap portable radio, and climbed to the top of the nearest hill in central Maine. There, he fiddled endlessly with the radio dial to reduce the static. There, he leaned into the speaker trying to decipher the unfolding story on the faraway radio station. There, he learned that his older brother had won the Boston Marathon.

A few years later, Gary ran a marathon or two himself. Then his life took him in other directions, and he was able to run little, if at all. Meanwhile, running remained a central theme in my life. The two of us grew disconnected by time and distance and inclination.

Fortunately, family has a way of regenerating itself. Twenty years later, several events caused us to begin having more contact with each other. Gary even got interested in running again, and we ran several short races together.

But nothing very long. Nothing like the 19 miles that now lay before us in the Boston Marathon. He must have been terrified. I was simply grateful. Any struggle is a thousand times easier when you have a partner.

We didn't say much in the ensuing miles. We didn't have to. But Gary was there, and his presence gave me new strength. He chased after Gatorade and PowerGel for me, encouraged me gently when I dragged on the hills, and pointed out every passing mile marker. One down, one fewer to go.

Eventually, we reached and crossed the finish line at Copley Square and fell into a brotherly hug. I thanked him for his help and told him I never would have made it without him. I would have been a former Boston Marathon champ dropping out of his anniversary race. Not even a footnote in the next day's news stories. But a failure that would have haunted me for years.

Six months later, the tables were turned. Excited and emboldened by his 19 miles at Boston, Gary decided to run the New York City Marathon. Since I had run New York many times and he hadn't run a full marathon in 25 years, I quickly volunteered to accompany him. I didn't want him to have to go the distance alone.

For more than 3 hours, we mostly breezed along. I pointed out the sights, Gary kept complaining that we should go faster, I kept advising that he should simply enjoy the experience and not worry about time.

Then at 24 miles, Gary "hit the wall" hard. His back stiffened, he couldn't lift his knees, and his stride shrank to about 6 inches. I looked often at his face, hoping to find a spark of energy, but there was none, and then I could look no longer. His face was too blank and frightening. Although I am older, he is physically thicker and more powerful than me, and I had always seen him that way. I had never seen him so weak, exposed, and helpless.

There was little I could do but fetch him water and energy gel, offer words of encouragement, and point out that the finish was getting ever closer. Exactly what he had done for me at Boston. So little but so much.

As we crossed the line, his legs buckled, and I

put his arm over my shoulder and dragged him to a medical tent for a brief massage. A couple of hours later, after a bath and a nap in our hotel room, he finally found the energy to speak. "I can't believe how hard it was at the end," he kept repeating. "I never would have made it without you."

Gary didn't have to say a thing. We aren't talkers, our family. But we are there for each other and always will be, no matter what the place or time or situation.

A RUNNER'S WORDS
OF INSPIRATION

Whole books have been filled with quotes about the running experience. Of course, the best quotes transcend running and provide lessons on life. Here are several that I have always responded to.

ON WHY RUNNERS RUN

"You have to wonder at times what you're doing out there. Over the years I've given myself a thousand reasons to keep running, but it always comes back to where it started. It comes down to self-satisfaction and a sense of achievement."

—STEVE PREFONTAINE,
American fourth-place finisher
in the 1972 Olympic 5000 meters

"The more I run, the more I want to run, and the more I live a life conditioned and influenced and fashioned by my running. And the more I run, the more certain I am that I am heading for my real goal: to become the person I am."

—GEORGE SHEEHAN, M.D.,
running philosopher,
writer, and physician

"What am I doing—nobody cares. It's just personal satisfaction."

—KENNY MOORE,
American fourth-place finisher
in the 1972 Olympic Marathon

"My life is a gift to me from my Creator. What I do with my life is my gift back to my Creator."

—BILLY MILLS,
Native American and winner
of the 1964 Olympic 10,000 meters

ON ACHIEVING GOALS

"Bid me run, and I will strive with things impossible."

—WILLIAM SHAKESPEARE

"Don't bother just to be better than your contemporaries or predecessors. Try to be better than yourself."

—WILLIAM FAULKNER

"Our greatest glory is not never falling, but in rising every time we fall."

—CONFUCIUS

"The harder you work, the luckier you get."

—GARY PLAYER,
South African golfing legend

"If one can stick to the training throughout the many long years, that willpower is no longer a problem. It's raining? That doesn't matter. I am tired? That's besides the point. It's simply just that I have to."

—EMIL ZATOPEK,
Czechoslovakian winner of the
5000 meters, 10,000 meters, and
marathon at the 1952 Olympics,
the only runner ever to achieve this "triple"

"Each of us must have a mountain [to climb], even if some might look on it as little more than a hill."

—GEORGE SHEEHAN, M.D.

"I like hills because you can see the top. I know that sounds glib, but you know that the hill is not going to keep appearing; it's there and once you get to the top, it's behind you, and you feel as though you have conquered something."

—ROB DE CASTELLA,
Australian marathon great and
winner of the 1986 Boston Marathon

ON THE SOLITARY
NATURE OF RUNNING

"The true competitive runner, simmering in his own existential juices, endured his melancholia the only way he knew how; gently, together with those few others who also endured it, yet very much alone. He ran because it grounded him in basics. There was both life and death in it; it was unadulterated by media hype, trivial cares, political meddling."

—JOHN L. PARKER JR.,
former American elite miler

"Stadiums are for spectators. We runners have Nature, and that is much better."

—JUHA VAATAINEN,
Finnish 5000- and 10,000-meter star
from the 1970s

"The true runner is a very fortunate person. He has found something in him that is just perfect."

—GEORGE SHEEHAN, M.D.

A Runner's Words of Inspiration

ON THE CONQUEST
OF MIND OVER BODY

"The human body can do so much. Then the heart and spirit must take over."

—SOHN KEE-CHUNG,
Korean winner of the
1936 Olympic Marathon,
when he had to use his Japanese name—
Kitei Son—to protect himself and his family

"Once you're beat mentally, you might as well not even go to the starting line."

—TODD WILLIAMS,
top American distance runner
and marathoner of the 1990s

"Ability is what you are capable of doing. Motivation is what you do. Attitude determines how well you do it."

—LOU HOLTZ,
famed football coach with
Notre Dame and the New York Jets

"In running it is man against himself, the cruelest of opponents. The other runners are not the real enemies. His adversary lies within him, in his ability with brain and heart to master himself and his emotions."

—GLENN CUNNINGHAM,
American mile great of the 1930s,
despite severe burns that nearly
cost him his legs in childhood

ON THE CHALLENGES OF COMPETITION

"Racing teaches us to challenge ourselves. It teaches us to push beyond where we thought we could go. It helps us find out what we are made of."

—PATTISUE PLUMER,
American Olympian
in the 1992 Olympics

"The will to win means nothing compared to the will to prepare."

—JUMA IKANGAA,
Tanzanian winner of the
1989 New York City Marathon

A Runner's Words of Inspiration

"I don't train. I just run my 3 to 15 miles a day."

> —JACK FOSTER,
> New Zealand masters great
> who ran a 2:17:28 marathon at age 46

"I'd rather run a gutsy race, pushing all the way and lose, than run a conservative race only for a win."

> —ALBERTO SALAZAR,
> American winner of the
> 1981, 1982, and 1983
> New York City Marathons

"Never really give in as long as you have an earthly chance."

> —ALF SHRUBB,
> British distance running great
> of the early 1900s

"A race is a work of art that people can look at and be affected by in as many ways as they're capable of understanding."

> —STEVE PREFONTAINE

"Fear is the strongest driving-force in competition. Not fear of one's opponent, but of the skill and high standard which he represents; fear, too, of not acquitting oneself well. In the achievement of greater performances, of beating formidable rivals, the athlete defeats fear and conquers himself."

—FRANZ STAMPFL,
Austrian distance coach who
guided Roger Bannister to the
first sub-4-minute mile

ON THE CHALLENGES
OF LONG DISTANCE

"These high, wild hills and rough, uneven ways draw out our miles and make them wearisome."

—WILLIAM SHAKESPEARE,
Richard II

"If people were possessed by reason, running marathons would not work. But we are not creatures of reason. We are creatures of passion."

—NOEL CARROLL,
Irish middle-distance star
in the mid-1960s

A Runner's Words of Inspiration

"You have to forget your last marathon before you try another. Your mind can't know what's coming."

—FRANK SHORTER,
1972 Olympic Marathon gold medalist

"I was unable to walk for a whole week after that, so much did the race take out of me. But it was the most pleasant exhaustion I have ever known."

—EMIL ZATOPEK,
after a marathon

"To describe the agony of a marathon to someone who's never run it is like trying to explain color to someone who was born blind."

—JEROME DRAYTON,
Canadian winner of the
1977 Boston Marathon

"I am too tired even to be happy."

—GELINDO BORDIN,
Italian winner of the
1988 Olympic Marathon

Simplicity

It is a gray, coldish November in New England, and I have just finished my fourth and last year of collegiate cross-country racing. It has been a good season, but also a long and tiring one, so I decide to reward myself with several months of simple, unfocused training.

I will keep running, of course, because I still have goals for the next spring. Most important of them: the Boston Marathon, which, as it turns out, is the one I will win.

But for the present, I have no immediate plans. I will run an indoor 2-mile race in mid-January, a good 2 months from now. Until then, I will do my usual daily workout, perhaps even two, with no thought other than to keep one foot moving in front of the other. I don't expect anything special to come of this, and I am amazed when it does.

Training is supposed to be extremely directed. Exercise physiologists and coaches have established what's known as the specificity of training rule. If you wish to conquer Mount Everest, you must practice hiking at high altitude. If you wish to succeed at the marathon, you must do many 20-mile runs. If you wish to run a fast 2-mile, you must dedicate yourself to hours of intense interval training—fast sprints on a track.

For the next 2 months, I do the opposite. I do *nonspecific* training. I wake up, I pull on my sweat clothes and running shoes, and I point my body out the door. Once outside, I don't pay any attention to intervals, hill repeats, long runs, tempo training, fartlek, or any of the dozens of specialized running workouts known to build speed or endurance. I just run at a comfortable pace. Nothing could be simpler than this.

Or more reinvigorating. As the weeks and miles flow past, I feel myself growing stronger. I don't fret about the lack of specific workouts. I don't worry about upcoming races. I am content to enjoy every run for the simple, relaxed hour that it provides me.

January comes soon enough, and I travel to Boston for the indoor 2-mile. There are only six of us in the race, and one is an Australian, the world record holder. The others are mostly Californians whose bodies look taut and tanned. They obviously haven't been running through snowstorms in layers of sweat clothes.

At the start, someone trips and falls. I instinctively leap over the somersaulting body and barely maintain my own balance. The rest of the race is a blur. I only remember that I have never felt so good, so energized in a race. And I have never run so fast.

As the laps blur past—we will run 22 of them in all on the wooden indoor oval—I manage to stick with the Aussie and the other tanned bodies. I have never run so light on my feet, never picked up my knees so effortlessly to launch the next stride. I seem to skim across the track like a flat rock on water.

Okay, I don't win, but that's almost immaterial. The Aussie and one of the California runners have faster finishes than I do, but I place third and run 8:45—about 20 seconds faster than I had expected. In a 2-mile race, this is a virtual light-year. I am thunderstruck.

This race taught me a profound lesson: The simple approach is often the best. As we enter ever more technical times, with ever increasing levels of complexity and decision making, we need to remember that the simple path can harness great powers.

During his much-read and discussed life at Walden Pond, Henry David Thoreau preached simplicity above all else. He felt that the unencumbered life was paradoxically the fullest.

Thoreau walked often and everywhere, mulling

over the day's options and ramifications. If he were alive today, I imagine he would be a runner, covering his favorite haunts at a steady jog. Not that walking wouldn't be part of his routine. But he'd also run because running is really just advanced walking; because it is more vigorous and, hence, healthier; and because it opens even more veins of creative and reflective thought.

Running has its roots in our prehistory. We don't run because Baron de Coubertin invented the modern Olympic Games in 1896, but because our survival once depended upon it and, to a lesser extent, still does. Millennia ago, small packs of early man stalked game for food on the plains of East Africa, chasing for a while, then resting, then chasing again until their hapless prey was exhausted and could escape no more.

Scholarly tomes and popular books have been written about the Paleolithic diet of these early humans—roots, nuts, seeds, grains, berries, and small amounts of lean meat—and what has happened when the modern diet changed to fats, sugars, and dairy products. The result: rampant heart disease, diabetes, depression, obesity, high blood pressure, and similar ills.

But little has been written about a correlate to the Paleolithic diet—the Paleolithic exercise program. Early man jogged and walked and then rested overnight, then jogged and walked again—in response to food supplies, local vegetation, and changing seasons. Today, for most Westerners, this is no longer the case. Exercise is no longer a part of daily life. And the result is the so-called lifestyle diseases.

We were meant to run, and we do so naturally when left to our own devices. Watch a group of children on the playground, in your backyard, or wherever they come together. When they play games like tag, they run for a while, with squeals of obvious delight, and then rest until they are recovered again. Run and rest, run and rest. It is the perfect exercise program because it is coded in our genes. It is what our forefathers did millions of years ago.

And it is also ridiculously simple—a child's game. Literally. Not to mention a powerfully effective training program, despite having no coaches or workout plans. In a similar way, my own running has often been best when I have left it alone, left it simple.

Life is complicated and never slows down. It seems only to get faster and more convoluted, with increasing things that need doing around the house. With family and friends. In the office. On weekends. Late at night, when everyone else is asleep. Early in the morning, before anyone else wakes up. Can we possibly cram more activities and responsibilities into our days?

My life gets as harried as anyone else's, and whenever it threatens to spin out of control, I simplify. I slow down. I focus on just several things, and one of them is always exercise. I eliminate everything else that's not absolutely essential. I remember Thoreau and a magical race in Boston, and I remind myself of the power of simple, concentrated activity.

Courage

THE POTENTIAL FOR GREATNESS
LIES WITHIN EACH OF US

When I was young, I thought courage began with a capital C. It always involved swashbuckling heroes who appeared in history books or adventure movies. Somebody usually died in these stories, but many others were saved by the hero's Courage. Without it, Freedom or Democracy or Independence or some other word that also begins with a capital letter would have been lost.

Growing up has changed my views on courage. I still honor our heroes, particularly those who have fought to sustain important ideals. But I've also come to believe that, more often than not,

courage begins with a small c. And it doesn't turn
into a major book or a Hollywood marketing cam-
paign.

In fact, courage is available to all of us. We
don't have to be standing on the precipice of history—at a time and place when momentous social
forces collide. We only have to look at ourselves full
face in the mirror. Most acts of courage do nothing
more than change the life of the person who sum-
mons it. Which, of course, is everything.

I have seen many acts of courage in running.
Indeed, the sport has a special appeal for those who
are looking to change their lives. While running at
first appears to depend on great physical strength
and endurance, it is, in fact, based almost entirely
on strength of mind. Those who have the will will
succeed.

I first met Linda Downes in New York City
more than 20 years ago. A victim of childhood
polio, Linda could have chosen to spend her life in
a wheelchair. Her legs were nearly useless. But she
refused to accept her 95 percent handicap, so she

made her way around New York City on crutches, under her own power.

I spent several days with Linda, riding the subways, attending college classes, negotiating stairways, and generally seeing the world in a way that able-bodied people rarely do. It took Linda endless, agonizing minutes to go up or down a flight of stairs, which, I suddenly realized, are *everywhere*.

Since Linda's legs didn't work, she got around by thrusting her crutches forward, planting them, and dragging her frail body forward. Her feet never cleared the ground. They made a loud "scra-a-a-atch." I'll never forget the sound of Linda Downes "walking." Like chalk dragged across a chalkboard, it left a chill.

At the end of each day, Linda went to track practice. A pioneering member of the Achilles Track Club, a running club for people with various handicaps, she had finished the New York City Marathon the year before and would complete many more. Linda had to start the marathon at daybreak—4 hours ahead of the big throng you see on TV—and she finished late in the day. But finish she did.

Oprah Winfrey never had to worry about a too frail body. Her problem, as everyone knew, always revolved around too much body. She was constantly trying to lose weight, and constantly losing the battle, until she met a personal trainer, Bob Greene, who believed in running and goal setting to lose weight.

Oprah's secret goal was to complete a marathon. Now, you have to understand, the world had never seen a less likely marathoner than Oprah. Fat, soft, female, black. Working incredibly long, hectic days. And far too famous to ever risk a marathon—the most open, public, and potentially embarrassing of athletic endeavors.

She decided to risk it, nonetheless, simply because the marathon had gotten inside her head, and she refused to let go. She *needed* to run a marathon, no matter what the odds and risks, to prove something to herself.

I happened to be attending the same marathon, the Marine Corps Marathon in Washington, D.C. And when word leaked out that Oprah was about to become "the most famous person ever to run a marathon," I figured I ought to run with her.

The next morning, I stood in the rain in a Pentagon parking lot waiting for Oprah. When she arrived, she didn't look at all like a glamorous TV star. Covered by an already soggy sweatshirt, she was just one more scared and shuffling runner among the 15,000. I fell into step a few yards behind her. (Many miles later, when someone told her that the editor of *Runner's World* was just behind her, she reached back to shake my hand.)

I've run nearly 100 marathons and seen many more, but I've never witnessed anything like that marathon. Two guys from the *National Enquirer* were running beside Oprah. They had been flown in overnight, along with a squadron of photographers, to stake out her hotel room from 4:00 A.M. on. And they had only one reason for being there: to catch

Oprah in an embarrassing failure moment that they could plaster all over their paper.

The marathon is tough enough without obstacles like that. Oprah also had to deal with thousands of other runners offering her a handshake, patting her on the back, wanting to chat for a few minutes. A gracious person, she met these interruptions with a smile and a thumbs-up.

For the first 18 miles. After that, she lost her strength. Needing every bit of energy and concentration she could summon, Oprah lowered her head and simply trudged forward. She knew that marathoners often "hit the wall" at 20 miles. She was getting ready for the battle of her life.

And she made it. She slowed down a little, but she never once walked. Oprah wasn't the most graceful runner I have ever seen—most runners aren't particularly graceful, that's reserved for Olympians— but she was incredibly determined, and that's all that really matters.

The Marine Corps Marathon finishes with a horribly difficult ½-mile hill to the Iwo Jima Memorial. It's a cruel thing to do to a marathoner—putting a big hill at the end—but it also seems to make the personal victory a little sweeter.

Oprah chugged up the final hill and under the finish-line banner to complete the marathon in a little over 4½ hours—a highly respectable performance, especially for a woman who had to deal with the press, her fans, and her fears every step of the way. Especially for a woman who knew that any success would be largely private, but any failure would be trumpeted in headlines around the world.

Oprah and Linda both succeeded because they understand about courage and change. Both qualities begin with a small c, but there's nothing small about their power or their ability to help you find a new direction. The longest journey begins with a single step. You only have to take that step. Remember: They did it, so can you.

A RUNNER'S ESSENTIAL READING

What follows is a sampling of books that have best helped to steer my running, shape my thinking, and spark my creativity.

LORE OF RUNNING, BY TIMOTHY D. NOAKES

I had heard about Tim Noakes, the South African researcher-writer-philosopher, for many years before I finally met him. When I did, I was most impressed by his blazing eyes. They radiate curiosity and invite debate. Noakes likes nothing so much as a good athletic controversy and cherishes nothing so much as the opportunity to give his opinion. Often, I've found, it's the best one available.

In his brilliant and wide-ranging 1991 book, *Lore of Running*, Noakes summarizes the literature to date on the mechanics of running, the physiology of training, and the psychology of competition. He shows readers how to analyze their own running and lifestyle to determine, and perhaps invent, the strategies that will take them to their goals. The outline of chapter 12, "Understanding Injuries," demonstrates Noakes's approach; here are subheadings such as "Virtually

All Running Injuries Are Curable"; "Treat the Cause, Not the Effect"; and "Never Accept as a Final Opinion the Advice of a Nonrunner." This book is sure to inspire any runner with half the curiosity of Noakes himself.

DON QUIXOTE DE LA MANCHA, BY MIGUEL DE CERVANTES SAAVEDRA

I first read the famous story of the knight on an impossible quest when I was a teenager about to become a marathoner. Did I see some of myself in the book? Sure. I felt then that I was setting out on the purest, most noble path available to a young athlete—one that would require total concentration and an ascetic lifestyle.

Okay, so Quixote lost touch with reality and began tilting at windmills. I did a few crazy things, too. But in the end, I achieved several goals that most runners never attain. And today, I have a clearer vision. I can see that running marathons is truly quixotic—idealistic but not very practical—and still worth the effort. We all need to pursue some noble and difficult-to-attain goals, or what's a life for? I know that I can't bring back the age of chivalry, but through running, I and millions like me can establish possible dreams and give them our best efforts.

THE COURAGE TO START, BY JOHN BINGHAM

John Bingham is well-known to readers of *Runner's World* magazine as "The Penguin," our back-of-the-pack correspondent. He represents a huge constituency of slow runners with humor and delight. *The Courage to Start* shows a deeper, more sensitive Bingham, a man attuned to the inner sadness and yearning of middle age. But Bingham joyously accepts the human condition, suggesting that simply rediscovering the potential for motion can restore optimism and improve our outlook.

This is a beginning runner's book, and much more. It has the training schedules and shoe information that one would expect. But *The Courage to Start* differs from other books and articles on beginning running because it never assumes that the runner wants desperately to get faster or thinner. Bingham finds that the run itself is often the best reward. "It is distance, not speed, that holds the answers. The reward comes with crossing and confronting the boundaries of fatigue. For these runners, satisfaction is measured in miles, not minutes." Bingham likes you the way you are, and he welcomes you to enjoy running with him.

THE ODYSSEY, BY HOMER

The classic Greek adventure story filled many weeks of my freshman year at college and has remained with me since. After helping to win the Trojan War, the hero Odysseus begins the long journey home to Ithaca and his beloved wife and son. En route, he encounters many obstacles, both horrific and beguiling, but his courage and resourcefulness eventually help him complete the voyage.

The tale is among the oldest we have, and still the lessons remain true today. Never have we encountered more fears, ranging from changing economies to corporate downsizing to certain terrible diseases that seem to be getting more prevalent. Never have we faced more temptations—fast-buck schemes and sweet, fluffy foods and digital revolutions. Never have we more needed to lead heroic lives that focus on the core values in our lives, particularly home and family.

THE ELEMENTS OF STYLE, BY WILLIAM STRUNK JR. AND E. B. WHITE

This tiny book looms large in the world of writers and editors (where I spend most of my time these days), but I dare say its teachings extend beyond publishing. Its pages argue passionately for the power of simple words and sentences. I imagine that I'm not the only reader who has extended the lesson to all of life, putting great stock in simple acts and values.

The Elements of Style is only 85 pages long, and the part I reread several times a year—"Elementary Rules of Usage"—spans just 33 pages. Here are 22 rules of the writing life, the most famous of which is rule 17: "Omit needless words." Explains E. B. White, who developed the book from a course his professor William Strunk Jr. had taught at Cornell University: "Vigorous writing is concise. A sentence should contain no unnecessary words, a paragraph no unnecessary sentences, for the same reason that a drawing

should have no unnecessary lines and a machine no unnecessary parts."

This rule does not limit us, for we can still fly high and
far if that's important to us. The rule simply insists that we
stay focused on our goals. When we stray too far, we lose
sight of the finish line.

RUNNING TO WIN, BY GEORGE SHEEHAN, M.D.

Decades ago, George Sheehan wrote a column for his local
paper, the *Red Bank Register*. He was the local eccentric, an
outgoing introvert, publicly musing on the strange pleasure
he took in long-distance running. The philosophical sayings
that form many runners' identities come from Sheehan and
from this early period.

Running to Win was published in 1992 and thus represents later Sheehan, a different, more scientific Sheehan who
has proof that his hobby is an important part of healthy
living. Unlike when he started writing, there were lots of other
runners around when Sheehan wrote this book, and this work

incorporates their knowledge and experiences. Here, you'll find solid advice on training, racing, and lifestyle as well as acceptable medical intervention. Sheehan the coach is every bit as straightforward as Sheehan the philosopher: His advice on preparing for hot-weather racing begins with instructions to overdress during the transitional days of spring. It's not fun, but it works, and that's always Sheehan's main point.

ONCE A RUNNER, BY JOHN L. PARKER JR.

In this 1978 book, John Parker succeeds better than anyone else at putting down on paper the real rigors and emotions of world-class running. That is why this book had to be a novel; no real person would allow a biographer to dissect his soul so completely.

Here are all the factors that swirl around inborn talent, setting that talent free or suppressing it, turning it into a gift or a curse. Parker's hero Quenton Cassidy has to seek out an environment that will be good for his running, moving around at the demands of his restless ability. Parker's description of

Cassidy's training demonstrates that excellence in running is nurtured on ever-increasing physical stress and pain. Cassidy sacrifices romantic relationships for the only relationships that matter—relationships with the training track and with other athletes, each of whom mentors a different facet of the upcoming runner.

Parker excels at painting word pictures of the interactions between runners, but doesn't overlook the side issues that concerned running in the 1970s. One of the most fascinating: the way runners discuss the then-forbidden under-the-table payments.

GÖDEL, ESCHER, BACH: AN ETERNAL GOLDEN BRAID, BY DOUGLAS R. HOFSTADTER

Is it possible to love a book that you don't understand? I think so. At least that's the only way I can explain my admiration for Hofstadter's first book, which won him the Pulitzer Prize in 1980. I picked it up at a bookstore, curious about the title, and grew more fascinated as I leafed through the pages. The thick book purported to find unifying themes among mathe-

matics, art, and music, including some of the great practi-
tioners of each (mathematician Kurt Gödel, painter M. C. Es-
cher, and composer Johann Sebastian Bach).

Not only that, but the very organization of the book
was different than any other book I had ever seen, from the
table of contents to all the sections within. Here was a writer
who dared to explore new territories. How exciting! I gave the
book to my 12-year-old son, already much smarter than I, and
he said that it changed his life. In fact, he wrote about it in the
college essay that helped him gain acceptance to Harvard.

Years later, I contacted Hofstadter and discovered that
he was a passionate runner—not a marathoner but someone
who used regular running to add order and rhythm to his life.
I shouldn't have been surprised. Running is full of basic patterns—from stride counts to breathing rates—and Hofstadter
has devoted his life to uncovering patterns in everything from
our thinking to our art.

A Runner's Essential Reading

Goals

Every youngster has a favorite children's book, and mine was *The Little Engine That Could.* I would ask my parents to read it to me every night, night after night. I remember how the engine struggled to huff and puff its way up the long slope, and how the driving, steam-powered pistons pushed it forward inch by hard-won inch. But most of all, I remember the engine's refrain: "I think I can, I think I can, I think I can."

Most runners hate hills. They see only the obstacles. They feel the burn in their chests and the heaviness in their legs. But for some reason, I've always liked hills. I see a challenge, a goal, and I feel instantly galvanized to achieve the goal. I think I can, I know I can, I simply have to stay on course and keep chugging along.

Running well on hills requires several key strategies, all of which work well in tackling any big goal. The first and most important, of course, is a positive attitude. The Little Engine had that, and many wise people have observed that you can't accomplish something if you don't believe you can. Or the converse: If you believe something is beyond you, it is.

Running hills also requires a physical adaptation. You can't run hills efficiently with the same stride you use on the flats. You need a shorter, more pistonlike stride. On hills, I actually pretend that I'm a steam engine: chug, chug, chug. I think I can, I think I can, I think I can.

Short strides work on the hills because they keep you close to the surface, pushing forward against it. True, you don't progress very far with each stride, but you make steady, gradual progress. And that's the key.

This technique has served me well on countless hills and several races up well-known mountains. The first was the 8-mile Mount Washington Road Race in New Hampshire. The race organizer had a favorite joke about this event: "It's an easy course—there's only one hill." We all chuckled. Standing at the starting line, looking up toward a summit shrouded in clouds, we didn't have much choice. Humor was definitely called for.

The clouds proved an advantage that I didn't realize at the time. Since I couldn't see the top of the mountain (and the end of the race), there wasn't much reason to look. That's always a temptation in hill running and in chasing after a dream. The effort is hard; you naturally want to see how much farther you have to go. Is your goal getting any closer? Does it seem that you can reach out and touch it? That would be great, that would definitely motivate you. And, goodness knows, we need all the motivation we can get to keep us working toward our goals.

The problem is that tops of mountains and long-sought goals don't move quickly into focus. They're far away, and the truth is that you're often not moving very fast. Chug, chug, chug. You could look up 100 times to check your progress, but the top of the mountain probably wouldn't seem any closer. The result is that you feel frustrated and discouraged, not motivated.

The solution, of course, is not to look—or at least to look as infrequently as possible. Stay centered in the moment. Look down at the road directly in front of you. Chug, chug, chug. Concentrate on the basic, essential things that you have to get done. Short stride, short stride, short stride. Time will pass more quickly and productively if you stay focused in the moment.

I did this on Mount Washington, and it worked. Before I knew it, I had passed through the clouds and reached the summit.

Running up the stairs of the Empire State

Building, which I have done several times, proved quite similar. You'd go crazy if you counted each floor as you passed it: 17, 29, 41, 54 . . . is there no end to this madness? Instead, I kept my head and eyes down and concentrated on my footwork to make sure I didn't trip. The 90-plus floors took care of themselves, and before long, I was bursting out into the cold February air and the finish on the Empire State Building's observation deck.

Pikes Peak presented a different challenge. The race was a full marathon, with the halfway point at the top of Pikes Peak. This meant I'd be spending more than 5 hours on the mountain. My powers of concentration are quite good, but this race was long enough and tough enough to demand a new plan.

I decided to take short walking breaks, to drink some water, and to eat some of the fig bars I carried with me. During these breaks, I also took a moment or two to enjoy the sweeping views. Sometimes you have to stop to smell the roses, right?

I figured that if I spent most of 5 hours staring down at the dirt and rocks under my feet, I'd miss a once-in-a-lifetime opportunity to appreciate the majestic Colorado mountain ranges. (Thirty years later, I haven't been back, so it was certainly a good decision.)

The lesson here: While you always have to stay focused on your goal, you also need to stay flexible enough to adapt to different conditions. When in the mountains, enjoy the mountain scenery. Nobody achieves his goal without having some fun along the way. Without fun, we'd give up long before the finish line. If there's any way to make the road easier and enjoyable, I'm all for it.

I didn't, however, look upward at the top of Pikes Peak. Instead, I concentrated my tourist views on the surrounding mountains that filled the horizon. I knew where I was headed, and I'd have plenty of time to enjoy the top once I achieved it.

I try to develop a clear picture of what and

where my goals are—otherwise, I'm certainly doomed to failure—and I have a firm strategy for getting there. But I don't check my progress every stride or every day. I simply stay the course and stay focused on the short-term realities. And, most important, I stay confident. I know that if I think I can, I can.

lesson fourteen
Children

WHY THEY MUST

CHOOSE THEIR OWN PATHS

All parents have favorite photos of their children, and I reach often for mine. When I look at these photos, dozens of memories flash through my head. Memories that remind me of things I should have realized about children but didn't for far too long.

For many years, I didn't understand how much I wanted, and expected, my children to be like me. I didn't pressure them, but I figured I was setting a good example, and they would naturally follow in my footsteps. This applied especially to my running. What could be healthier? Why wouldn't they mimic me? I felt certain they would and, in so many different ways, truly wanted them to.

As it turned out, they had different plans. And the force of will to find their own ways.

Laura, the younger of two, will always be Daddy's little girl, and she bears the mantle well. There's almost nothing that Laura doesn't handle with grace and aplomb. She seemed that way almost from the moment she was born: happy, smiling, energetic, fun to be with.

Laura and I did endless things together: skipping hand in hand up the street, learning to ride a bike, driving to the local ice cream shop for a certain essential food. And when the big local road race passed in front of our house, I had no trouble convincing Laura that she should stand there and cheer for me.

In fact, I set her up with a table, a water jug, and a collection of paper cups so she could hand water to the passing runners. She couldn't have been happier. This was like playing house and watching a parade at the same time.

An hour later, we road racers came churning past. For some reason, a local newspaper photographer happened to be there, and he caught the perfect moment. Laura is standing at the side of the road, 4 years old, looking adorably cute in a pair of coveralls. She's holding out a cup of water just the way we had rehearsed it.

In midstride and running quite fast, if I do say so, I reach out to grasp the cup. But my momentum forces me to slap the cup hard, and water sloshes upward in an arc that catches Laura by surprise. She looks startled. Snap! The photographer takes his shot, and it's all there: the small girl, her helping hand, the eruption of water, the shocked little face.

When I saw this photo in the paper the next day, I looked for symbolism, and found plenty. It seemed only a matter of time before she would be running cross-country and maybe entering road races. I imagined the great times that father and daughter would have.

I probably focused on Laura because anyone

could see that her older brother, Daniel, had no interest in running. Quiet and introspective, he
amused himself with his own thoughts, his imagi-
nary games, his Lego block constructions.

Daniel caught an atypical pneumonia when he
was 4, spent nearly 3 weeks in a hospital, and suffered lung scarring from the illness. After that, he
simply couldn't keep up with his friends when they
were playing tag, soccer, hide-and-seek, or any
other active games. Soon he gave up trying. He pre-
ferred to glide back and forth by himself on the
front-yard swing, oblivious to cold, wind, and other
distractions.

I tried endlessly to get Dan to jog around the
block with me, to ride a bike, to strap on a pair of
roller skates, but to no avail. These were all things I
had done with my dad when I was a child, and I
mourned silently that I couldn't now do them with
my own son. Not that I ever quit trying. I just
couldn't make myself stop.

I suspect I also didn't pay enough attention to
those areas where Dan clearly excelled. His Lego

constructions were amazing—vast and complex—but I hardly noticed them in the corner of the living room. I wonder now if I praised him enough for all the reading he did or for the journals he wrote in school or for the way he could fill page after notebook page with equations and battle strategies and planetary alignments.

After Dan's mother and I separated, I wasn't there all the time, and Dan made the best of it. He started lifting weights in the basement, he joined the swim team, and he soon progressed from the slowest swimmer on the team to the fastest. He captained the tennis team and began devoting himself to the martial arts. Meanwhile, he kept reading and writing and solving equations, and soon gained admission to Harvard. You couldn't imagine a nicer, more talented, more physically and mentally developed person.

During one of the summers of Dan's high school years, we vacationed together in California, and I took my favorite picture of him. We are down at a rocky patch of shoreline in Big Sur country, and

Dan has discovered a rushing rivulet with a fallen tree trunk over it. He decides to walk the trunk to the other side.

At first, it's slow, edgy going. Dan moves forward inch by cautious inch. But halfway across, he finds his footing, turns toward me, stands tall, grins, and throws both arms out to his sides. Snap! The photo shows a confident young man, perfectly balanced between two shores, fully capable of making his own way. At least that's my interpretation.

Much as I once wished it, my children have never run a road race and may never. They have simply grown into the people they were meant to be. Laura was president of her high school class 4 years in a row, a top player on the *boys'* tennis team, and now attends a fine eastern college. She and Dan are both complete miracles to me.

I believe both have achieved their unique successes because I eventually learned to get out of their way. It didn't come easily—not to this dog-eared, determined road runner who has gone through his life grinding out 1 mile after another and thinking it a pretty good prescription for everyone else.

As it turned out, my kids didn't lack for goals or for the discipline to achieve them. Otherwise, they wouldn't have ended up where they have. So maybe I taught them some basic lessons.

But they taught me much more. They showed me, conclusively, that we are all very different. We all have unique passions and unique paths. Which is why parents can't be cookie cutters. We can't *mold* our children into ourselves or anyone else. We have to let them run free to discover themselves. It's the greatest gift we can give them.

New Year

I am not much of a reveler. No one has ever called me a party animal, and I can't remember any time when I was the last person to leave a bar or a late-night function. This morning, however, I seem to be surrounded by party animals, and, admittedly, I'm acting a bit like one myself.

Yes, morning. It's a few minutes before noon on January 1—any January 1—for I have passed my New Year's Days in the same way for more than 2 decades. We gather in a neighborhood in Mystic, Connecticut; we jog 5 miles to the shore; and we plunge into the freezing waters of Long Island Sound.

The New Year is barely 12 hours old, and we have already found a symbolic way to celebrate. Others watch football and munch chips all day long. I prefer to rage against sloth and proclaim my zest for life, action, and renewal.

In 1969, I made the plunge with two other friends. We had such fun that we did it again the next year and the next, a few others joining each year. When local TV and newspapers caught wind of our frolic, the group quickly doubled and tripled. In a few more years, we reached 100, then 300.

The January 1 Run-Swim, for lack of a better name (or, in truth, any name at all), is a deliberately disorganized event. There has never been an entry form or an entry fee. No one wears a race number. It just happens. Spontaneity is the order of the day.

Indeed, we enforce only one rule: No one is allowed to win. On this day, we must all run together, champions and chubbies, greyhounds and penguins. The entire group moves at the pace of the slowest runner. The rest of the year will be competitive enough. Let this one run be pure togetherness. We relax and take the time to chat with new friends. Most of all, we catch up with old acquaintances.

You couldn't find a happier or more diverse group of people. The high school boys are stripped to their shorts, despite the 40°F air temperature, displaying "Happy New Year" written on their chests in thick, black marker scrawl. The high school girls are wearing polka-dot bikinis. More than a handful of us appear to have just left the previous evening's parties. Several are talking about the *Runner's World* Midnight Run in Central Park; they have driven in from Manhattan.

I am wearing a dime-store Hawaiian lei—don't ask me why—and blowing on a cheap noisemaker. My wife wears a sparkly, cardboard tiara. There is always a small bottle of peppermint schnapps being passed from hand to hand. Some years I feel like imbibing; others, I don't. I can never predict which.

I like to drift to the back of the pack and view the wild throng from behind. Today, there's no hurry. The pack always reminds me of a caterpillar, the way it pulses and throbs and moves slowly ahead. I can also imagine the transformation into a beautiful butterfly. This is January 1, and the year has such potential. The future is so alluring.

When we reach the shore, all hell breaks loose. Now everyone has license to dash for the waves. The kids sprint faster and scream louder than anyone else, somehow managing to run and pull off their sweat clothes at the same time.

We more experienced swimmers continue at our leisurely pace. We know the ocean will not recede. It will still be there when we arrive, a minute or two after the younger set. No hurry.

On the beach, I like to count my blessings. There are so many, and the timelessness of sand and ocean always reminds me of my good fortune. Not that I tarry and ponder for long.

The wind is biting cold, and the water must be confronted. I pull off my shoes and sweatpants, remove my glasses, and reach for a hand—my son or daughter, my wife or nephew. Then I sprint across the beach and into the waves, letting loose a primal whoop (it seems to lessen the shock) and taking my annual baptismal plunge.

The run, the water, the plunge, even the cold—they have taken on greater meaning for me than I could ever have imagined when we began this rite back in the late 1960s. I could write a sermon, I'm sure, to describe all the levels of meaning. But the biggest and most important is also the most obvious: This is a new beginning.

Life goes on, day after day, but it also has the ability to reinvent itself, to start over. This is what the seasons show us. We all have marveled at the apple tree's ability to rest through a dark, cold winter, then to grow new leaves in the spring, to blossom again, to bear fruit.

We don't often think of our own lives this way, but I think we should. Each year holds such potential for new beginnings. We runners know this because we tend to measure ourselves according to our age. Races have age-group competitions, and I know people who have won their age-group in a particular race as a teenager, and then again as a twenty-something, a thirty-something, a master (over 40), and so on.

But it's not the winning that's important. It's the starting over. It's the seeing things afresh, through new eyes and a different mental outlook. We all have the capacity for this if only we'll take it.

Change can be frightening, let's admit it. I am scared sometimes when I think about all the years I have lived, more than half of a lifetime. I would love to have some of them back. Oh, if I were handed a couple of decades, I would cherish them so. I would give every moment the honor and respect it deserves.

But I know this can't happen, so I need a different outlook. And the one I choose is the seasonal approach. I try to think of myself as an apple tree. Time is not linear, it moves in circles. Come spring, I will bloom again.

To live this way, I must act this way. I must develop many different rites and passages and symbolic events. Regeneration is hard work, like everything else. It doesn't just happen. You have to believe it first. Then you must enact it.

After diving into the water, I surface quickly and gasp for air. Birth. I'm sure I scream louder than any newborn child, but I'm shivering too hard to hear it. I turn back to shore, my knees churning, my hands flailing at the water. I can't move fast enough. A biting wind claws at my neck, stifling the urge to continue screaming.

I feel the water get shallower under my feet. In a few seconds, I'll emerge from the icy, dark waters. But right now, in truth, I'm enjoying the moment. I feel unbelievably refreshed and reenergized. This is, indeed, a primal new beginning. Now I'm truly ready for the New Year.